D1569461

THE VIRGINIUS AFFAIR

THE VIRGINIUS AFFAIR

Richard H. Bradford

FOREWORD BY WALTER LAFEBER

COLORADO ASSOCIATED UNIVERSITY PRESS

Copyright © 1980 by Colorado Associated University Press
Boulder, Colorado 80309
International Standard Book Number 0-87081-080-4
Library of Congress Card Catalog Number 20-520000
Printed in the United States of America
Designed by Bruce Campbell

For Mary

Contents

Foreword xi

Preface xv

Acknowledgements xvii

ONE   The Beginning of War 1

TWO   Republicans, Yankee and Spanish 17

THREE   The *Virginius* 25

FOUR   Death to Rebels 39

FIVE   A Nation's Righteous Anger 57

SIX   Madrid 75

SEVEN   The Thanksgiving Protocol 87

EIGHT   The Mechanics of Compromise 97

NINE   Burial at Sea 109

TEN   Aftermath 115

ELEVEN   Conclusions 129

    Notes 141

    Note on Sources 165

    Index 175

List of Illustrations

Frontispiece: the *Virginius* at sea.   ii
From *Harper's Weekly,* November 29, 1873.

1. Hamilton Fish as secretary of state.   3

2. Daniel Sickles, minister to Spain.   19

3. The soldier of fortune Ryan and his three Cuban   32
   comrades.

4. Joseph Fry, the ill-fated captain of the *Virginius*.   34

5. Artist's conception of the capture.   42

6. Sir Lambton Lorraine, whose timely arrival   50
   halted executions.

7. H.M.S. *Niobe* at anchor in Santiago Harbor.   55

8. The sinking of the *Virginius* off Cape Fear,   113
   North Carolina on December 26, 1873.

9. A Thomas Nast cartoon of the contretemps   116
   between Fish and Sickles.

10. Caleb Cushing, who succeeded Daniel Sickles   121
    as minister to Spain.

Foreword

When our descendants can finally view the twentieth century
with adequate perspective and some detachment, they will
probably conclude that it was significant less for its world
wars and space ventures than for its revolutions. They might
even decide that the revolutions were important causes of
those wars and moon landings. In 1900 a half-dozen im-
perialist powers owned or otherwise operated nearly all the
globe's profitable areas. Now, as the century moves to a close,
long-developing nationalist revolutions in Austro-Hungary,
Southeast Asia, Africa, the Middle East, and Latin America
have joined radical revolutions in Mexico, Russia, China,
Cuba, Iran, and Nicaragua to transform the political map.

These upheavals have presented United States officials
with their biggest headaches. A comprehensive history
of twentieth century American foreign policy could be organized around consecutive chapters detailing the United
States's attempts to deal with revolution: the Cuban (1868 to
the present), Chinese (1900 to the present), Mexican (1911
to 1941), Russian (1917 to the present), Vietnamese, Chi-
lean, Iranian, and since 1956, African. In nearly every one of
those instances U.S. officials tried to control, stop, or rollback
the revolution through some kind of intervention. In all the
instances except the last three, Americans deployed military
force, and the chapters on those three are not yet completed.

Washington's attempts to control the revolutionary aspira-
tions of other peoples have not been notably successful. The
lack of success has been due in part to the natural limitations
of rationally-applied military or economic power when it has
to deal with a passionate, seemingly irrational drive to freedom. But it also has been due to the deep historical roots of
those revolutions that Americans seldom glimpsed — roots so
deep that they nourished revolutionaries generations later, so
deep that they were impervious to American or European attempts to eradicate the branches.

The Cuban revolution had such roots. It is the story of the

(xi)

first six years of that struggle, and the American response to it, that Richard Bradford tells. He has focused his account on a crisis in 1873 when Spanish officials in Cuba seized the *Virginius* and executed most of its American crew on the grounds that they were pirates who supported Cuban revolutionaries. Bradford tells this fascinating story succinctly and well. American diplomatic history is not awash with important books on the 1870s; apart from several works on Secretary of State Hamilton Fish, few other analyses of the period have attracted much attention. Yet this is an important era, and one of Bradford's contributions is to uncover the domestic interest groups (some of them so corrupt that they lowered even the moral level of that uncommonly decadent decade), bureaucratic wrangling, colorful personalities, and emerging international forces that shaped those years.

The *Virginius* episode so well combines fascinating personal stories with events of international significance that one wonders why it is only now being told in detail and supported with the necessary research in Spanish and British as well as American sources. One explanation might be that it was a revolutionary-caused crisis in which the United States did not intervene. It remains a quiet exception in our post-Civil War history and stands in stark contrast to the American invasion of Cuba in 1898 that aimed at driving out the Spanish rulers—and stopping an increasingly radical Cuban revolutionary movement.

As Bradford emphasizes, such an invasion did not occur in 1873 for a number of reasons. Following Allan Nevins's 1937 biography of Hamilton Fish, historians have usually viewed the aristocratic Secretary of State as the primary restraint upon President Ulysses Grant's single-minded, and often simple-minded, ambitions in the Caribbean. Bradford's portrayal of Fish, however, is more complex than Nevins's. The secretary of state had no immutable rules against American imperialism (he had been a Northern expansionist in the 1850s), and his decision not to move into Cuba in 1873 was shaped by a host of political forces that Bradford analyzes.

Among those forces were three that receive special and overdue attention: the Spanish political situation, the splintering of Cuban society and politics, and the diplomatic role played by Great Britain. It is now clear that the British were pivotal in working out the settlement. The importance of their involvement ramifies, moreover, for it demonstrates that the historic rapprochement between the United States and England accelerated as early as the 1870s when the peaceful adjustment of the *Alabama* claims arising out of the Civil War was followed by the beginning of England's understanding—if not always approval—that United States power was moving inexorably southward.

The *Virginius* affair was an occasion when the tragic execution of the crew, an excited response by American "yellow journals," revolution just off U.S. shores, economic disasters at home, corrupt officials in Washington, and an impetuous General in the White House should have combined to produce United States military intervention. Bradford explains why that did not occur, and does so in a work that should become the standard account. In our own era when revolutions (including the Cuban) continue to run their course, when Americans—frightened that their own nation's preeminent power is slipping—must deal with those upheavals, and when U.S. foreign policy is often shaped by shadowy domestic interest groups, the *Virginius* crisis deserves this close restudying.

Walter LaFeber

Preface

"My Father, Miss Hope, was a filibuster, and went out on the *Virginius* to help free Cuba, and was shot, against a stone wall."[1] Thus the hero of Richard Harding Davis's 1897 novel, *Soldiers of Fortune,* replies when the heroine inquires of his past.

Readers of the 1890s would have recognized immediately the name *Virginius*. It had been headline news twenty-five years before when the ship, carrying arms and men to aid the Cuban fight for independence against Spain, was captured by a Spanish cruiser. Many of the men aboard, supposedly American citizens, were shot in Santiago de Cuba. It was, for a brief moment, a *cause célèbre*.

In the nineties, as relations between Spain and the United States deteriorated over the Cuban question, the story of the *Virginius* was revived. Cuban propagandists and their sympathizers in the United States used it to demonstrate Spanish perfidy and cruelty. Some saw the *Virginius* crisis as a lost opportunity to teach Spain a lesson and to wrest the island from Spanish domination.

In 1906, Harry Thurston Peck wrote, "For the war with Spain Mr. McKinley deserves neither praise nor blame. The conflict had been inevitable ever since the Cubans rose in 1868. . . and since Spanish soldiers shot down the crew of the *Virginius* at Santiago. From that moment, Spain and the United States were like two railway engines heading toward each other upon a single track. A collision between them could not be avoided."[2]

If the United States and Spain were on a collision course during the administration of Ulysses S. Grant, the *Virginius* affair offered the same opportunity as a railway switch. It could have been used to allow the two nations to collide or could have been thrown to prevent collision and hope that time would allow them to change course and preserve the peace. As it happened, the fateful clash between Spain and the United States was averted for another quarter of a century. Secretary of State Hamilton Fish is credited with preventing war in 1873, but

PREFACE

other forces operated to help resolve the conflict. Some of these influences were domestic political matters, but one source of support rested with the policy interests of Great Britain. Had not the Foreign Office been interested in preserving peace between Spain and the United States, war might have occurred in spite of the best efforts of Fish.

To contemporaries then, the crisis was an important event in late nineteenth century diplomacy. Those effects, however, and the crisis itself have never been thoroughly studied. Aside from Allan Nevins's massive biography of Hamilton Fish, and a careful account by French Chadwick as part of his study of Spanish American relations, the affair, although still recounted in most texts on diplomatic history, is one of the forgotten episodes in the foreign relations of the Gilded Age.[3]

This study concerns the manner in which peace was preserved for a generation. That feat allowed America not only to avoid bloodshed but also to concentrate on internal development without the handicap of wars and empires dividing its attention and energy.

Acknowledgements

In the course of research and writing any scholar incurs obligations. My thanks to the numerous library and archival staffs in the United States, Great Britain, and Spain who were consistently courteous and helpful; to Sir John Murray for permission to use the Layard Diary in the British Museum; Viscount Wimborne generously gave permission to make use of the Layard papers. Thanks to Shannon Husley for kind help at a crucial moment during my research. Professor Walter LaFeber of Cornell University provided aid and encouragement at a difficult time. Professor Robert H. Ferrell of Indiana University, after serving as my advisor when this work was in the dissertation stage, then showed unfailing kindness and Olympian patience in helping with several successive drafts. Most important, my wife Mary has been editor, proofreader, and typist on this work. It is to her credit that unlike its namesake this *Virginius* completed its voyage.

CHAPTER ONE

The Beginning of War

THE *Virginius* affair of 1873 boiled up suddenly. After some weeks of apparent indecision it subsided. And yet in long retrospect—over a century to the present day—it appears to have been one of the more remarkable, although perhaps least remarked, events of American history in the post-Civil War era. It was remarkable because of the danger it presented to the decent ordering of the nation's foreign policy, the danger of a war between the United States and Spain over Cuba; the country was barely past the Civil War, with all of that conflict's dissensions, and the time was not right for another war. The affair received little attention from chroniclers of the nation's past because, happily, the country did not go to war. The triumph of Secretary of State Hamilton Fish slipped into that special limbo reserved for what in fact may be the greatest achievement of statecraft, the prevention of trouble rather than the contriving of some splendid conflict.

The *Virginius* affair occurred in the middle of the two presidential terms of Ulysses S. Grant. Even before the commencement of this ill-fated presidency there were premonitions of its course, and by 1873 its confusions and corruptions were evident and its place in history virtually predictable. The reputation of the Grant administration was perhaps cast at the President's inaugural ball, held on March 4, 1869, an affair that began as a triumph and turned neatly into a social disaster. On that gala evening thousands of ticket holders had swarmed into the Treasury Building for a night of merrymaking. Old-line society ladies from New York and Boston, dressed in Paris gowns, mingled with daughters of the American frontier dressed from the shops of St. Louis and Chicago and in some cases in homespun gowns of their own devising. No one cared that the Chief Executive would not be present at his own ball—it was said he was a poor dancer and even worse on small talk. Voices could be heard damning

(1)

Senator Charles Sumner of Massachusetts for thwarting the original plan to hold the festivities in the Capitol. But it was whispered that a man whose wife had deserted him could not bear the thought of so many people enjoying themselves. The dance floor became crowded. At first no one minded a bit of pushing. Then as hours passed the heat turned stifling, gentlemen grew short of temper, corsages wilted, new gowns began to look as faded as the dancers' spirits. By refreshment time the floor was so mobbed that movement was impossible. When guests began to struggle into the supper room, the initial polite movement toward the food turned into a rush. Ladies lost their escorts. Finally, after the food disappeared, after more dancing, people had had enough, and the throng started toward the cloakroom. There the dancers discovered the disaster of the evening. The crush became so great that hundreds of persons could not obtain their wraps and had to trudge home in cold March weather with nothing more than gowns and suits to protect them from the wind and slush.[1]

Grant's acts as President dampened the enthusiasm of his supporters the same way the weather destroyed the dancers' spirits—his inexperience in politics inspired one scandal after another. Then, beginning in 1873, financial panic beset the business of the entire nation (admittedly not because of great wrongdoing in Washington, for the depression of the 1870s was world-wide). Worst of all, Grant seemed not to understand what was going on during his presidency.

Whatever successes were achieved in foreign affairs during the general's time in office took place because of the work of a six-foot-tall gentleman from New York of leonine appearance, who stepped off the train in Washington's station two weeks following the inauguration, to take office reluctantly as secretary of state. Hamilton Fish was Grant's third choice to head the State Department. Sixty years of age, he was a one-time member of the Whig party, who had enjoyed a distinguished career as a lawyer, member of the House of Representatives, governor of New York, and senator. His only experience with foreign policy had come while on the Senate Committee on Foreign Relations during the early 1850s. Ironically, in view of his later problems as secretary of state, one of the main difficulties in foreign policy had been the

1. Hamilton Fish as secretary of state. From Allan Nevins, *Hamilton Fish, the Inner History of the Grant Administration* (New York: Dodd, Mead & Co., 1937).

South's acquisitive attitude toward Cuba. This desire Fish, like most northern Whigs, opposed.[2] In 1858 he had withdrawn from politics; there then seemed no place for him. During the ensuing war he was of course too old for military service, but had done his best as a private citizen to aid the Union against the rebellious South, speaking and writing in support of the Lincoln government. After the end of the war there still seemed to be no place for him in politics. An aristocrat by temperament, he did not fit the freewheeling era of American history after Appomattox known as the Gilded Age. He was a quiet, self-contained man. A contemporary remembered that he was "not a talker particularly, but he was powerful."[3] Much to his surprise, and that of the nation, Fish in 1869 had been appointed secretary of state, apparently because during the election campaign he had entertained Grant in his house in upstate New York and the general had taken a liking to him.

Fish inherited a Cabinet department that had seen enlivening and even great days under his predecessor, William H. Seward, but was beginning to come on hard times even before that other New Yorker had left office. The very location of the department in 1869, a former orphanage out on Fourteenth Street, removed from other government offices, pointed to the declining importance of foreign affairs in American life. There was some possibility that the State Department might be abolished; with the successful laying of the Atlantic cable in 1868 some people had suggested that the nation might not need consuls and ministers, for heads of government could communicate directly with each other.[4]

Fish knew better than to think he could deal with foreign governments by putting himself at one end of a cable. None of the problems of his era as secretary of state was susceptible to so easy a solution. He was especially concerned about relations with Great Britain. The United States government after the Civil War was determined to extract monetary compensation from the British government for its unneutral or at least incautious behavior during the Civil War, and eventually in 1872, after arbitration at Geneva, the British paid. The British were necessarily touchy about this diplomatic defeat, and no amount of talk over the Atlantic cable was going to make things much easier. Fish knew he would have to be careful with his transatlantic cousins.

But the most difficult diplomacy during Fish's tenure involved relations with Spain over the course of a revolution which the Cubans had raised up against the Spanish in 1868, before Fish had come into office. Here careful diplomacy proved necessary for ten years until the war's close in 1878, after he had left office.

Americans had long been interested in what the Spanish were wont to describe as the Ever Faithful Isle. More than a century earlier, in 1762, during the French and Indian War, troops of Britain's North American colonies had occupied Havana. Years later President Thomas Jefferson had turned a covetous eye toward the Spanish island when he wrote in 1808 that annexation was "exactly what is wanting to advance our power as a nation to the point of its utmost interest."[5] For a President who simultaneously was risking his country's unity over the Embargo, this was an overstatement, but Jefferson did make it. For the next half century American concern for Cuba centered first on the possibility that weak Spanish control of the island might give way to possession by Britain or France, a change of ownership that could constitute a far greater threat to the United States than would any action by the declining monarchy of Spain.[6] A second reason for United States interest in Cuba was cupidity—the attractiveness of the island.

Hope of obtaining Cuba had increased markedly in the 1850s when some Americans sought to expand the nation's territory and simultaneously extend slavery. The idea that attracted many Americans of the time was that their country was a young country, as compared to the effete monarchies and empires of Europe, and because of its youth was naturally going to inherit lands in the Western Hemisphere, perhaps even all of the Hemisphere, which inheritance would result, so contemporary writers alleged, in a "more perfect" Union. Some of these enthusiasts of Young America, as noted, were interested both in the extension of slavery and the perfection of American geography. Safeguarding the South's peculiar institution virtually dominated the concerns of the Democratic Party under President Franklin Pierce.[7]

(5)

Even before Pierce entered office a Cuban patriot, Narciso López, had gained support among Americans for a revolution in Cuba, particularly in the American South where he secured the financial aid of slaveholders and support of young adventurers who signed up for his expeditions. In the last of these invasions, in 1851, López was captured, and the Spanish publicly executed him along with several Americans in the great square of Havana.[8] But in 1854 the Cuban issue rose up again in American politics as well as foreign policy when James Buchanan, then minister to Britain, and two other American envoys met in Aix-la-Chapelle to consider how the United States might obtain Cuba after Spain rejected an offer to buy the island. In a confidential dispatch to the State Department, later known as the Ostend Manifesto when its contents became public knowledge, these three expansionists recounted that if Spain refused to sell Cuba the United States should steal it. Buchanan became president three years later. Perhaps fortunately, sectional conflict at that time was becoming very serious, allowing the Cuban question to recede.[9]

Meanwhile the Cubans were beginning to take more interest in their own independence. During and immediately after the American Civil War the yearning for independence in Cuba increased rapidly as a result of the uneasy social situation on the island.[10] In the early nineteenth century, at the time of South America's wars for liberation, Spain had received the loyalty of Cuba, but loyalty was more a result of lack of opportunity than an expression of affection. Dominating island society then and later were the Peninsulars, Cubans born and brought up in Spain who after reaching adulthood had returned to live mainly in the towns where they enjoyed the privilege of ruling over the Creoles (Cubans of Spanish descent, born in the colony). While the Peninsulars had only a new-found interest in the island, Spanish law and custom favored them over the Creoles for positions in the government, the professions, and the army. Not much involved in politics were the many blacks and mulattoes. Cuba was one of the last places in the Western Hemisphere, along with Brazil and Puerto Rico, to maintain the institution of slavery. For years after the American Civil War, several hundred thousand black and mulatto slaves toiled on the island's sugar plantations, creating wealth for Cuban and Spanish masters.[11]

What was an unhappy social situation was complicated by the Madrid government's restrictions on trade. Perhaps because Spain's empire had been born in the age of mercantilism, restrictions on Cuban trade continued long after the theory of mercantilism had passed into disfavor among the statesmen of northern Europe. Cuban affairs actually were not impossible, so far as concerned trade. Even with the Spanish tariff, exports from the United States to Cuba in 1855 reached $8,044,582. But the restrictions were onerous.[12]

Spain levied a disproportionate share of taxes on the Cuban planters, as compared to taxes on other parts of Cuban society, especially the Peninsulars. Gradually the idea of revolution—of freedom—took hold in the minds of patriots. As early as 1854 a British traveler observed that "Cuba is at the present politically in a critical and alarming condition and the most intelligent natives and resident foreigners live in constant dread of a terrific and sanguinary convulsion."[13] After the American Civil War increasing agitation in favor of cutting Cuba's imperial tie came from a "Republican Society of Cuba and Puerto Rico." Founded by exiles in New York in 1866, it circulated a pamphlet entitled *Voice of America*. The Society defied both Spanish rule and the institution of slavery by calling for "liberty without distinction of race and color."[14] In the island a *Partido Reformista* or Reform Party appeared in spite of the fact that parties were illegal. The government of Queen Isabel II formed a commission in 1866 to study the Cuban question, raising hopes of Cubans who noted the membership of such liberals as José Morales Lemus.[15] The next year, in 1867, Madrid levied new taxes. The Creoles were verging on revolt.

Revolution broke out on October 10, 1868 when thirty-eight Oriente landowners met at the plantation of Carlos Manuel Céspedes near Yara where the Indian hero Hatuey had died fighting the Spaniards in the sixteenth century. They heard Céspedes proclaim independence. They charged Spain with continuance of slavery, excessive taxes, and deprivation of political, civil and religious liberties.[16]

In the early stages of the revolt Céspedes became the leading figure. Born in Cuba and educated in Barcelona, he had agitated for independence in Spain, in exile in France, now in the island. Nothing if not a complete patriot, the same day he announced independence he freed his slaves and brought them into the revolutionary army.[17] He directed his ragged force to some early victories over Spanish troops. The revolt gained momentum, and a provisional government of the Republic of Cuba appeared at Bayamo. By October 17, 1868 an American living in Manzanillo wrote Secretary Seward that "Rumor of a contemplated rising of the natives of. . . this island headed by some eight or ten estates owners who were known to be highly dissatisfied with the late taxation imposed on landed properties and their production is confirmed."[18]

The Spaniards at first did not take the threat in the eastern provinces seriously, but as the revolt spread the captain general of Cuba, Francisco Lersundi, sent a force supported by artillery to take the rebel capital of Bayamo. More important for future relations between Spain and the United States, he created the Volunteers—(Voluntarios), a corps somewhat like a national guard. The Volunteers proved of high importance in the subsequent course of the revolt.

The actions of the Volunteers on occasion appeared incomprehensible, and yet made perfect sense to the Volunteers. They clearly were on the side of Spain—if that side meant putting down the rebellion. Their work, and they were effective at it, was to garrison towns, leaving the army to patrol the countryside. But they were essentially against the new republican government that had toppled Queen Isabel II and abolished the monarchy in 1868. In January, 1869 this government had recalled Captain General Lersundi and replaced him with the liberal General Don Domingo Dulce, who received orders to reform the Cuban government so as to bring it more into line with the interests of the Creoles. The Volunteers did not want such changes. Their ranks comprised mainly of recent arrivals from Spain who had come to the island for adventure and money, they wanted to make their own individual fortunes and liked things as they were. Moreover, as individuals mostly without money they believed that the Creoles looked down upon them. In their own wisdom they decided that the rebelling Creoles needed to be put down with brutality. In editorials in their newspaper, *La Voz de Cuba*, they made clear that they would accept no compromise with the rebels. To prevent Cubans from joining the rebellion they guarded all entrances to Havana and other towns and executed anyone without a pass. Cuban women were mistreated for allowing their hair to fall over their backs; the Volunteers called this a coiffure *a la Céspedes*, after the revolutionary leader. On pain of death they forced passersby in the street to shout *Viva Espana!* On January 22, 1869 they learned that performers at the Villanueva Theater were insulting the Spanish flag. More than two hundred Volunteers entered the theater and suddenly poured volley after volley into the unsuspecting audience, leaving dozens of people dead, dying, or severely wounded.[19]

One insane act led to another. Volunteers fought not so much for Spain as for their special cause. They broke into the palace of the new captain general and ordered him out of the country.[20] His departure in June, 1869 set a pattern for years to come. Each governor became virtually a prisoner, his tenure at the pleasure of the Volunteers. The Madrid government, unable to reimpose order, accepted this arrangement.

All the while the Spanish army was behaving with similar brutality. A decree from Dulce on February 12, 1869 had ordered all insurgents captured with weapons to be shot. Immediate execution was the sentence for captives of low rank, while more prominent individuals met public death by the garrote.

Brutality begot brutality. At first the insurgent Cubans did not retaliate but set Volunteers or Spanish army prisoners free. In August, 1869 one of the rebel commanders, Manuel Quesada, attempted to bring the Spanish army to an agreement on policy for prisoners. Rejection of this effort led him and the other rebel leaders to a policy of retaliation.[21]

During the early months the insurgents, as mentioned, had gained some successes over the Spanish, but then their cause seemed to lose momentum, and their small forces began to resort to guerrilla warfare. When at the outset of the fighting they lost their capital they established a new head-

(9)

quarters at Gúaimaro where they assembled and chose Céspedes as president of the republic and Quesada as
commander-in-chief, wrote a constitution, and formed a congress.[22] In the mountains in the eastern provinces the rebels
were secure, and there the provisional government held
meetings and printed money, even as did the government in
Madrid. The revolt nonetheless failed to spread westward toward Havana. The insurgents could not defeat their well-
armed adversaries.[23] The rebels began to operate in small
units, continually changing sectors. When troops searched
for them it was pursuit of a will-o-the-wisp. If the Spanish
army saw the enemy at all (except when walking into am-
bushes) it was through field glasses, a far-off band of
mounted figures carrying rifles and spears, riding under the
banner of a silver star set in a red background. An exhausting
search might produce one or two runaway slaves to be taken
back as prisoners to the accompaniment of cheers and
vivas.[24] In avoiding large-scale encounters the insurgents
strove to make the civil war too costly for Spain to oppose it.
They cut railway lines, blew up bridges, and, when Spanish
engineers rebuilt the bridges, blew them up again. They
wantonly burned sugar plantations. Shots would be fired in
the night, and figures bearing torches would move through
the cane fields and fade into the blackness, leaving overseers
or owners dead, and crops in flames.

It was of course not long before citizens of the United
States began to become sensitive to the fighting. Many Cubans held dual citizenship, from both Spain and the United
States, for during the López troubles nearly twenty years before not a few patriots, neglecting to notify the Spanish government, took the precaution of filing an intention of becoming American citizens. Some had lived only a few months in
the United States. They spent their lives in Cuba, holding offices to which only a Spaniard was eligible. But they could
call on United States protection. Early in the war it became
obvious to the American government that it was important to
define the status of naturalized citizens, for Spain was arresting Cubans as insurrectionists who claimed United States
citizenship.[25] In several instances Volunteers shot Cubans
who claimed such citizenship.

(10)

The colonial government in Cuba was doing its best to antagonize the government in the United States. Local authorities levied fines of increasing severity against American sea captains for slight infractions of regulations. One captain was fined $500 for not having a duplicate cargo list.[26] The situation of Americans in Cuba became perilous. At a review of Volunteers in Santiago cries of "Death to the Yankees!" punctuated the martial music.[27] Volunteers threatened the life of the acting consul in Santiago who in letter after letter was begging the State Department to send a warship to protect himself and local Americans.[28]

The great hope for the rebels was intervention by the United States. Céspedes and Quesada needed money. A few Latin American nations had recognized their government, but such diplomatic relations meant little to the men of Guáimaro so long as Spain controlled the sea. In the United States fugitive Cubans established *Juntas* in New York, Washington, Boston, Philadelphia and Tampa. The one in New York, known as "Central Republican Junta of Cuba and Puerto Rico," was the most important. Under its leader, José Morales Lemus, it raised money for the insurrection by sponsoring concerts, and holding mass meetings, as well as issuing bonds in the name of the infant "Republic of Cuba."[29] It hired a West Point graduate and former officer in the Confederate Army, Thomas Jordan, to recruit men and launch military expeditions against the island. Soon after the war began the Junta attempted to persuade the Grant administration to proclaim a state of belligerency in Cuba and recognize the independence of the rebels. They found allies among some American politicians and businessmen who for reasons of idealism and profit were anxious to see the government intervene even at the cost of war with Spain.

The insurgents were aware that intervention could make the difference between success and failure, but a split was developing between those favoring radical goals and those striving for moderation in the revolution. The radicals called for an immediate end to slavery and were equally opposed to membership in the Spanish Empire or in the American Union. The moderates on the other hand, who were particularly strong in the *Juntas,* were made up of men like José Morales

(11)

Lemus who had been Creole landowners and slaveholders. They wanted only gradual abolition of slavery, disapproved of social revolution and favored annexation by the United States. Thus one insurgent general looking to "the shining beacon of all nations" asked that Cuba be annexed. In August, 1869, the consul in Santiago told the State Department that "barbarous civil strife" made "the more enlightened Peninsulares desire annexation to the U. States should the Spanish government not be able to subdue the rebellion." He was convinced that the eastern provinces of the island would vote for annexation.[30]

Hope centered on the figure of Grant's thin, pale secretary of war, John Rawlins, an expansionist who in a speech in 1867 had said that he looked forward to the expulsion of all European powers from the Western Hemisphere. He had been Grant's chief-of-staff during the Civil War, and then had exerted a strong influence. During the subsequent presidency observers had believed he would be an *éminence grise*. Rawlins was a poor man, with family responsibilities and debts, a fact that did not go unnoticed by agents of the Junta who offered him $28,000 in Cuban bonds, which would remain worthless unless his government ensured the independence of Cuba. He accepted the bonds. The Cubans did not need to bribe him to obtain his support, however, as he was eager to commit the United States to what he regarded as a righteous fight.[31]

At the time that Rawlins was enrolled, support in the United States was increasing markedly. The House of Representatives on April 10, 1869 passed a resolution advising the President of its support if he wished to recognize a state of belligerency.[32] Grant was disposed to do so. He did not much care if such an act might lead to serious trouble. War with Spain had considerable appeal to Americans, for by religion, history, and politics the two nations had little in common and perhaps a good deal in opposition. Spain was almost entirely Catholic, a religious difference keenly sensed, for the America of the early post-Civil War years was already feeling the effects of an immigration that was predominantly Catholic. The founding of America had come as a result of bigotry in Europe; Protestant Americans of the nineteenth century could not forget the religious oppression that drove their ancestors out of Europe. The noted historian Francis Parkman, sympathetic to the Jesuits of New France, had no compunction in 1865 in describing the typical Spaniard of the sixteenth century as "bigotry incarnate." His fellow historian William H. Prescott was accustomed to Spanish cruelties in the conquest of the New World. John Lothrop Motley in his epochal volumes on the rise of the Dutch Republic celebrated the persistence of Dutch Protestants in the fight against Catholic Spain. An anti-Spanish bias penetrated such contemporary novels as Charles Kingsley's *Westward Ho;* its author ardently believed in the Black Legend which characterized Spain as the most cruel of all nations. Americans regarded the Spanish government as monarchical and absolutist; Spaniards, they were convinced, were the backwash of European civilization.[33]

It was difficult work to keep the country neutral. Everything looked toward intervention. In the summer of 1869 the State Department took an initiative in the Cuban question by sending an American businessman to Madrid to arrange Cuban independence in exchange for an indemnity of not more than a hundred million dollars, a sum the United States would guarantee. The proposal of this private American citizen, Paul Forbes, came to naught, for the Spanish demanded that the Cuban rebels first must lay down their arms, something the Cubans would not do. The leading personage in the Madrid government, General Juan Prim, who favored a sale, was assassinated.[34] In August, 1869 President Grant was preparing to recognize a state of belligerency in Cuba and left a signed proclamation to that effect with the secretary of state. Fish put the document aside while the President went on holiday in New Jersey. Late that month, John Rawlins died of tuberculosis, opening the door for Fish's influence in the Grant Cabinet to grow.[35] Recognition of belligerency was allowed to die during the current congressional session.

The beginning of the year 1870 saw an upswing of pro-Cuban sentiment when the Foreign Affairs Committee under the House of Representatives leadership of Nathaniel P. Banks of Massachusetts reported out a resolution urging the recognition of Cuban belligerency. During the previous year

Banks had written that "I want to identify my name. . . with the acquisition of the Gulf of Mexico as a sea of the United States." He was certain that every European country soon would "withdraw from this continent." He viewed Secretary Fish as a cold, aristocratic Anglophile with "nothing American in his policy."[36] But Fish carried the day, against the House resolution, by bringing Grant into opposition. If the President did not go along with him in making a stand against a recognition of Cuban belligerency, said Fish, he would resign.[37]

The reasons for Secretary of State Fish's constant opposition to recognition of Cuban belligerency have been much discussed. Fish's son-in-law, Sidney Webster, was legal counsel for the Spanish government in New York. Contemporaries and later Cuban historians believed the secretary's conservative temperament also disposed him toward Spain.[38] As a businessman Fish favored the interests of Americans who had invested in sugar and slaves and perhaps stood to lose if the revolution succeeded. Also if the State Department recognized belligerency, it would allow the Spanish to escape responsibility for damage done by the rebels to American owned property. There is some evidence that Fish believed the revolution would exhaust both sides, resulting in acquisition of Cuba by the United States without a war.

Fish was not alone in opposing Cuban belligerency. The "hard-money elite" of upper-class Northeasterners in both parties fought Cuban recognition with the same fervor with which they resisted soft money and supported civil service reform.[39] Among Republicans in the Senate, from his position as chairman of the Senate Committee on Foreign Relations, Charles Sumner dominated foreign policy questions. Attorney General E. R. Hoar and E. L. Godkin, editor of *The Nation,* together with Democrats Caleb Cushing and Manton Marble, editor of the *New York World,* were a mixture of pro-Spanish and anti-Cuban tendencies. All were part of an intimate circle with the secretary of state. As one critic of Fish admits, "Given the influence of this group, if Sidney Webster had never existed, Fish would probably have kept the same Cuban policy."[40]

The pro-Cuban faction on the other hand was somewhat

(14)

unsavory. It included New York's Mayor A. Oakey Hall, a member of Boss Tweed's ring, Charles A. Dana, vitriolic editor of the *New York Sun*, and the flamboyant Brooklyn Minister Henry Ward Beecher. Pro-Cubans within Grant's Cabinet tended to be such ex-Democrats as John Rawlins, Postmaster General A.J. Creswell, and the president himself, who could be swayed by the last person to whom he talked.[41] These men were not the remnants of the Southern Democrats who coveted Cuba in the 1850s; Cresswell, for example, although an expansionist held harsh views toward the defeated South, and Rawlins opposed annexation. One could perhaps say that they were "Young America" now reached middle age.

Legally and diplomatically Fish could make a good argument for denying recognition to the rebels. Spanish-American relations, he knew, sailed in the wake of the *Alabama* claims of the United States against Great Britain. During the Civil War, Britain in May, 1861, possibly prematurely had recognized the existence of a state of belligerency between the United States and the Confederate government. This move had allowed the Richmond regime to construct warships in Scottish yards. When one of those vessels put to sea and changed its name to the C.S.S. *Alabama,* it sank many United States merchant ships and became the object of a prolonged hunt by the United States navy before meeting its end off the coast of Cherbourg. Among Americans, Britain's responsibility for the *Alabama*'s damages had become an object of heated controversy during and after the war. The analogy between the Confederacy and Cuba was close. Fish knew the United States could not do the very thing vis-à-vis Cuba for which it had condemned Britain. Secretary Lord Clarendon had carefully noticed this situation in 1869 when he wrote that "The Spanish government may consider itself lucky that. . . the United States government. . . if it had not been afraid to damage its case with us would long since have recognized the Cuban insurgents as belligerents."[42] The Cuban revolutionary regime, moreover, deserved acknowledgment far less than had the Confederacy. The Cuban rebels were a small group, controlling no ports, no organized armies, whereas the Confederacy based in Richmond had

(15)

possessed all the accoutrements of national power.[43]

Such was the reasoning of the secretary of state against recognition of Cuban belligerency. By the summer of 1870 an observer of the Washington diplomatic scene might well have decided that if Fish could maintain control of events there would be no untoward action between the American and Spanish governments concerning a few rebels in rural Cuba. But the course of events often depends on small developments. The control of large matters of diplomacy can slip through the hands of the best of public officials through some unforeseen change in circumstances. Secretary Fish was about to reexperience this ancient truth about the precariousness of all human affairs, personal or public, national or international. While Fish sought to hold off any moves for Cuban recognition, lesser officials of the government of the United States dealt with more trivial matters, such as the question of getting rid of surplus ships left over from the recent war. In the lower reaches of the American government an opportunity arose to sell an erstwhile Confederate steamer which took up space in the Washington Navy Yard. A certain John F. Patterson bought the ship for $9,800.[44] For the Cuban Junta it was a promising investment. For Fish this transaction would mean nothing but trouble, and indeed serious trouble.

CHAPTER TWO

Republicans, Yankee and Spanish

A MONG Hamilton Fish's unpleasant tasks in the State Department was the distribution of patronage to deserving Republicans, for the spoils system ruled American politics, and even a gentleman like Fish found it necessary to huddle with politicians to decide who would share in the spoils of office. There was no lack of applicants for posts. Fish complained to a Senator that

> If German Consulates were to rain down for a month, there would not be enough of them to satisfy the studious Americans who wish to study German, the invalid Americans who wish to improve their health, the patriotic Americans who wish to serve their country, the ambitious Americans who see a future of greatness through the gimlethole of a consulate, the innumerable body of German-Americans who wish to revisit the "Vaterland," to say nothing of the professional officeseeking Americans, native, naturalized and neither.[1]

Fish often found himself disagreeing with Grant about the merits of appointees, but seldom did he disagree so completely as when Grant proposed Daniel E. Sickles for the legation in Madrid. There were sound reasons why Sickles should not represent the United States, and Fish meant to bring them up, but when the subject arose in a Cabinet meeting shrewd old Rockwell Hoar, the attorney general, raised objections first. "If I recollect aright," Hoar said in his Yankee drawl, "Sickles was connected with the Ostend Manifesto. I don't know how that would do in connection with his appointment to Spain." Fish sided with Hoar. Rawlins came down in favor: "Well I was in favor of the Ostend Manifesto myself at the time it was issued." Postmaster General John Creswell likewise remembered his own support of the Manifesto. Typically silent while this exchange went on, Grant ended the matter. "Gentlemen, I believe I was in favor of that Manifesto myself at the time it was issued." Sickles became minister to Spain.[2]

Sickles's indulgence in the affairs of Tammany Hall, and also in affairs of the heart, had made him one of the more criticized men of his era. Friendship with James Buchanan had led to a post in the London legation in 1853-1854 during the latter's tenure as minister. While in London, Sickles kept his eye on the voters back home and played the game always popular with American politicians, "Twisting the British Lion's Tail." Rumor circulated that he had presented a prostitute to Queen Victoria under the name of one of his political enemies. It is certain that he refused to toast the Queen during a banquet because Victoria's health rather than President Washington's memory was first on the list of toasts, and this act raised an uproar. Sickles liked to strut about the legation in the gaudy uniform of a New York militiaman. Buchanan liked him personally but knew Sickles was damaging the legation's work. He sent him back to Washington carrying dispatches, and then cautiously asked for his resignation. Sickles complied.[3]

Sickles in 1856 won election to the House of Representatives at the same time that his patron Buchanan was elected President. Soon he and his pretty young wife Teresa were appearing at dinners in the Executive Mansion. Sickles had every reason to expect political advantage to come his way. He seemed a man to watch, if he could learn discretion.

Characteristically he threw his advantage away by a rash, even insane, act when early in 1859 he learned that his wife was having an affair. The man in question was Philip Barton Key, district attorney of Washington, and the son of Francis Scott Key. Philip Key was considered the handsomest man in Washington, but Teresa Sickles had another reason to be unfaithful to her husband, for under an assumed name Sickles regularly had been boarding a train for Baltimore to meet his own light-of-love in a hotel. Through an anonymous note Sickles was informed of Teresa's infidelity. Consumed by rage, he armed himself with a pistol and went searching for Key. Meeting him in Lafayette Square, within sight of the Executive Mansion, he shot and killed the unarmed man. A

(18)

2. Daniel Sickles, minister to Spain. From *Dictionary of American Portraits* (New York: Dover Publications, 1967).

sensational trial followed. With the leading American lawyer, Reverdy Johnson, pleading his case, the jury acquitted Sickles on the grounds of temporary insanity, but his peers and public brought in a verdict of guilty, and his political future seemed ruined. For a social creature like the Congressman, fond of meeting companions for dinner and champagne at Delmonico's and of patronizing the theater, the ensuing social ostracism was a cruel punishment.

The Civil War offered an escape, yet also created a problem or two, even if it led eventually to the Madrid appointment. After raising a regiment, Sickles fought at Gettysburg where he lost a leg to a Confederate cannon ball. His skill in self-advertisement made him a hero to some, but acquired for him many enemies who tried to discredit his military ability and especially his role at Gettysburg. After the war Sickles remained on active duty as a major general in charge of the military district of North Carolina. For this patronage he could thank his connections and his wartime friendship with General Grant. The latter's election to the presidency in 1868 brought new opportunities. First came an offer of the legation in Mexico but Sickles rejected it. Then Grant tendered the Spanish post. For a moment it appeared Sickles would not accept because President Andrew Johnson in 1868 had approved an act providing that army officers who accepted nonmilitary missions must forfeit their commissions. Sickles would rather have foregone the Spanish assignment than give up his stars. Not until Grant assured him that because he was a retired officer and would serve without army pay in Spain, and thus not be required to give up his commission, would he agree to the post.[4]

A politician-general was not the best representative for a government to send to another government with which it was having problems, and indeed the leaders of Spain seemed at first unsure whether to regard the general's presence as an insult or a challenge. Sickles's talents were those of the intriguer rather than negotiator. He was accustomed to living in style, and soon was ordering wine and champagne from Paris, suits from London, and sterling silver spoons with the monogram "S" and a star on each side.[5]

It was the good fortune of Sickles's country that able assistants in the legation could supply the patience and tact he lacked. The first of his helpers in Madrid was young John Hay, already something of a poet and novelist, later to be secretary of state, who soon exchanged diplomacy for journalism by taking a position with the *New York Tribune*. Another young man, Alvey Augustus Adee, took over in September, 1870 as secretary of the legation. Later he would be an almost permanent assistant secretary of state, serving in that office without interruption from 1879 to his death (in office) in 1924. Adee had no awe of or illusions about the Tycoon, as he called Sickles. After a change of housing he wrote a friend, "Have taken rooms with young Napier, son of ex-minister in Washington, who when a little boy, playing in the street, once saw one man shoot another. Curious isn't it, how oddly things work about—now, after all these years he again sees Sickles and is brought in frequent intercourse with him." Adee's prose combined terseness and clarity, and throughout his long subsequent career he would show a rare gift for stylistic imitation that allowed him so to merge his style with that of a superior that it was impossible to tell where one writer left off and the other began, an invaluable asset in working for a minister absent as often as was the general.[7]

Sickles had never limited himself to official duties, and the Madrid legation quickly proved no exception. His duties were to deliver protests over seizures of American property in Cuba and against slavery and the Cuban war. But a whirlwind of energy like the general needed diversions. He moved easily in Spanish society, occupying the best box at the theater, attending the most noted dinner parties. Fluent in Spanish, he continued his intriguing, this time with the Spanish Republicans of the Cortes, who were then plotting to overthrow the monarchy of King Amadeo—which they soon would manage to do. Teresa Sickles had died before his coming to Spain, and her demise gave him additional license in his private affairs. American travelers sent Fish letters chronicling the minister's loose way of life.[8] Twenty years earlier the general had known Isabel II, the dissolute Queen of Spain, who now lived in exile in Paris. Sickles renewed the acquaintance. He became a frequent passenger aboard the Madrid-Paris express and rumor circulated about an *affaire de coeur*. Meanwhile in 1872, perhaps to put down the scandal, he married a Spanish young lady, Caroline de Creagh.

After his second marriage Sickles returned to the United States on extended leave as agent for the European investors in Jay Gould's Erie Railroad. Gould had been watering their stock, in a manner more outrageous than was considered acceptable by American railroad entrepreneurs. Sickles was so successful in his efforts against the unpopular Gould that the New York newspapers gave him much favorable publicity, and his clients presented him with a large fee and a fine house at 23 Fifth Avenue. He considered remaining in New York. With his ill-concealed disdain for King Amadeo, and his association with the Spanish Republicans, Sickles had succeeded in making himself *persona non grata* to the monarchical government. It was an open secret that Republican leaders had met at his house in Madrid.[9]

Prime Minister Don Mateo Sagasta could be forgiven for considering a request for Sickles's recall. The American minister must have known that he might be given his passports if he returned but he was not one to back away from a fight. Characteristically, he viewed Sagasta and the monarchy as enemies. He would return to Spain. His intentions now merged with Fish's plan to induce the Spanish government to negotiate seriously over Cuba. Fish ordered Sickles to carry a letter of recall and gave him specific instructions. If the Spanish proved truculent he was to inform them that were he to be recalled he might not be replaced. Fish hoped this threat of severing relations might be the dash of cold water required to bring the Spaniards to their senses and to a settlement of the long-standing problem of Cuba.

Spain's politics then came to Sickles's diplomatic rescue when the Spanish government became a republic. Cabinets and governments changed with amazing speed after the liberal revolution of 1868, and by 1873 many Spaniards asked, "Who is he?" when a new minister took office. Amadeo of Savoy, brought in by General Prim in an effort to establish a new monarchical house, saw the futility of his mission and abdicated on February 12, 1873, and his departure left a vacuum which, with Sickles's encouragement, the Republicans rushed to fill. Sagasta fell from power, and by the time Sickles reached Madrid there was a new foreign minister, Christin Martos, a Republican. Sickles was the most welcome envoy in Spain. Even Secretary Fish could momentarily forget his displeasure with his minister's nondiplomatic activities amidst the promise of a Cuban settlement, and wrote that "I congratulate you on your triumph over Sagasta. You remain—Where is he?"[10] Soon Sickles was walking between rows of troops presenting arms, a band playing the Star Spangled Banner, to inform President Estanislao Figueras that the American republic extended recognition to the Spanish republic.[11]

Far from solving problems, the republic in 1873 flooded the country with new crises and Sickles quickly grew weary of the government he had been proud to consider his creation. The foreign office continued to assure Sickles that the Cuban rebels would be defeated, impounded American property released, and a policy for freeing the slaves instituted. Five years of promises, since 1868, still were not being translated into deeds. Even if the government wished to adhere to its pledges there was little a republic could do. The Republicans were struggling against impossible odds. No sooner was the republic established than the backers of Don Carlos, the pretender to the Spanish throne, invaded northern Spain intent on taking advantage of the new government's instability. Supported by many Spaniards who preferred monarchy to republicanism, the ultraconservative Carlists plunged Spain into civil war forcing the government to withhold troops desperately needed in Cuba.[12]

The Spanish essayist Azorin pinpointed the republic's weakness when he wrote, "In addition to. . . the Carlist war and the war in Cuba, it had to cope with supporters who were republican only in name."[13] There was a disturbing lack of continuity in the republican cabinets that would have taxed the patience of more stable nations. No president or cabinet was in office long enough to become familiar with the duties of government, not to mention asserting authority over the country. Dissension within the party threatened to turn the republican experiment into chaos. All Republicans nominally held the same principles, but, in fact, substantial differences divided them. The moderate Republicans led by Emilio Castelar shared a bourgeois liberal outlook, a hatred of hereditary monarchy, opposition to clericalism, and a defiance for the Church in politics. They favored gradual change. Francisco Pi y Margall's wing of the party yearned to carry out more radical theories of government.[14] When Pi assumed the presidency his extreme federalist ideas brought disastrous consequences. In the summer of 1873 every town that wished to be an independent canton took the president's ideas literally, with the result that a flurry of revolts against the government broke out. The most serious rebellion took place at the naval base at Cartagena where mutineers from the fleet declared the town's independence. The general sent from Madrid to crush the rebellion took command of it.[15]

With Spain falling into a chaos similar to that in Cuba, Emilio Castelar defeated Pi y Margall for the presidency by 133 votes to 67 in the Cortes in September, 1873.[16] President Castelar was forty years old. Slightly above middle height, stout, with a chest of splendid proportion, Castelar had the build and voice of an opera tenor. He was, however, an orator. He loved order, shuddered at anarchy, and regarded stability as the primary condition of government. He was determined to suppress the federal insurrection. This was the individual who presided over the Spanish government when in November, 1873, a crisis arose in relations between the United States and Spain.[17]

CHAPTER THREE

The Virginius

THREE years before the Republicans took over the Spanish government, General Manuel Quesada arrived in Washington, on March 1, 1870, sent by his brother-in-law Carlos Manuel de Céspedes, president of Cuba's provisional government, on a mission to create a "financial, naval and military" center to aid the insurgents. Not quite thirty years old, Quesada had been a revolutionist during the López era, and when forced to flee the island had become a soldier of fortune in the army of Benito Juárez fighting the French invaders of Mexico. By the time the Cuban war broke out he had achieved the rank of general.[1] His task in 1870 was to devise a way around the detectives hired by the Spanish mission in the United States and around customs agents intent on enforcing American neutrality. He hit upon a plan to outwit both groups. His associates were two United States citizens, a father and son, Marshall O. Roberts and J. K. Roberts, owner and manager respectively of a steamship line in New York. The Robertses were also interested in Florida railroads and the Cuban revolution. The plan was to purchase a vessel named the *Virgin,* docked in the Washington Navy Yard.[2]

The *Virgin* had been constructed for the Confederate navy at a shipyard on the Clyde in 1864 and intended for a career of blockade running. A sidewheel steamer over two hundred feet long, ten feet from waterline to deck, with a displacement of four hundred ninety-one tons, and remarkable speed, it was an ideal vessel for navigating along a coast to land men and supplies. It made several trips between Havana and Mobile, through the blockade, before capture by Union forces. For the next five years ownership of the vessel passed back and forth between the United States and private shipping interests.[3]

Then came a fateful development. In August, 1870, the *Virgin* was sold to John F. Patterson for $9,800. On the surface he was the owner of the *Virgin*. In reality he was the agent of Quesada and the Robertses. The three men had bought the steamer with money furnished by the Junta, although Patterson's name alone appeared on the bill of sale.[4]

By September the *Virgin* was steaming to New York under command of Captain Francis Sheppherd, and about two weeks after arrival, the captain learned from J. K. Roberts that the owners of the vessel were the Cubans Manuel Quesada and José Maria Mora, and that they intended to use the ship in the insurrection. Roberts inquired if Sheppherd would be willing to command the expeditions. Hoping to obtain more information, the latter visited Mora's house that evening. Quesada and Mora declared themselves the owners. Sheppherd accepted command with the understanding that he would act under Quesada's orders and that the ship was to land men and supplies for the insurgents.[5]

While the *Virgin* lay in New York Harbor, Patterson and J. K. Roberts had the vessel overhauled, and registered it under the name of the *Virginius*. Patterson took an oath that he was sole owner. At the same time that he was committing perjury, a legal oversight occurred which later reinforced the *Virginius*'s status as a ship without a country. American law required that an owner "and one or more sureties" should give bond to the United States government to the sum of $2,000 prior to a ship's registry. Patterson and Shepperd alone executed the bond on September 26, without the necessary sureties.[6]

The *Virginius* cleared New York on October 4, 1870 on its first mission for the insurgents, and a few miles below Sandy Hook intercepted the tug *Virginia Seymour* carrying General Quesada and twenty insurgents who climbed aboard with their gear.[7] A couple of weeks later, in the Caribbean, the *Virginius* rendezvoused with the schooner *Billy Butts*, out of New York, towed the schooner to a secluded island, and there took on a cargo including several hundred cases of ammunition and four brass howitzers.[8]

During the next two years the *Virginius* fully qualified for the name of "outlaw" that the Spanish applied to it. Sheppherd initially headed for Puerto Cabello, Venezuela, where a civil war raged between the adherents of one Guzman Blanco and those of his opponent. While the vessel lay at anchor the sailors rowed Quesada to a point some miles down the beach for a meeting with Blanco, while the steamer openly flew the flag of Cuban insurrection. When he returned, Quesada announced to Sheppherd that he had made an agreement to aid Blanco, with the understanding that if successful the Venezuelans would aid the cause in Cuba with men and arms. This was too much for the captain. Angered over what he considered a breach of contract and also because he had not received the salary promised him, he left ship and returned to New York. All the while the Cubans, flying both the American and insurgent Cuban flags, aided the Venezuelans by transporting troops and fighting some bloodless duels with enemy schooners. When the conflict ended in a victory, Blanco, true to his word, sent a small force with Quesada to Cuba. Making a landing at Bocco de Cabello on the island's southern coast the expedition reinforced the Cuban rebels with arms, men, and burros, which earned this particular operation the nickname of *Expedicion de los Burros*. The Cuban forces of insurrectionist General Maximo Gomez took the field with renewed hope.

The ship's movements thereafter became cloudy, until April, 1872, when at Aspinwall, Columbia (present-day Panama), Quesada prepared another expedition for Cuba. A new skipper came aboard, in the person of Francis Bowen, an experienced captain attracted by wages of $300 monthly with promise of a $5,000 bonus if successful in landing the expedition. On assuming command Bowen had as his first task the purchase of an American flag. Although six Cuban flags were in the *Virginius*'s locker, no American flag was aboard the American-registered ship.

The proposed filibustering expedition from Aspinwall did not turn out well. Neither Bowen nor Quesada made any attempt to disguise the vessel's operations. About sixty Cuban soldiers barracked near Aspinwall. Supplied by the steamer, they awaited transport. On May 1, under sealed orders from Quesada, the ship weighed anchor. The Spanish man-of-war *Pizarro,* also in Aspinwall, threatened to seize the rebel steamer, and by order of the local American consul the U.S.S. *Kansas* escorted the *Virginius* to sea.[10] But the Cubans made it only as far as Puerto Cabello, its rendezvous of two years before, where the vessel remained, leaking badly and out of coal.

During the next months in 1872 the Cubans engaged in complicated maneuvers which only served to prove to anyone who had doubts that the *Virginius* was owned and operated by the insurgents. On one occasion Quesada signed a bond for $10,000 for the ship's indebtedness without making any attempt to communicate with the supposed owner, Patterson. Each captain who came aboard, and there were several, learned that Quesada and the Junta were the owners, and that the ship would not be returning to the United States. Believing the Junta's cause might be safer under British colors than the Stars and Stripes, Quesada entered into a scheme to sell the *Virginius* to a cooperative British subject. The sale was completed; the *Virginius* remained in the service of the Cubans. But protection under the British flag failed, sunk by a broadside from Her Majesty's local consul who, the day after the sale, called upon the current skipper, Captain Charles Smith, and asked if he intended to hoist the British flag. When Smith replied "Yes," the consul quietly added, "I have a telegram from the British minister at Caracas to seize her as a pirate if she hoists the British flag." The banner was never unfurled, and the Cubans managed to have the sale, which legally "ransacked" all prior titles, nullified, and title restored to Patterson.[11]

During this maneuvering the American minister to Venezuela, William A. Pile, noted the suspicious character of the vessel in communiqués to Fish. Most consuls in the ports the *Virginius* entered seemed under no illusion as to its operations and, indeed, were carefully informed of the character of the ship by the Cuban owners and American captains. They refused to listen to Spanish complaints and seemed eager to assist the insurgents. Even Pile maintained that he found nothing that would establish bad faith, and consequently decided to "treat the vessel as with any other American vessel," except to exercise more than usual care at seeing the craft safely out to sea, away from annoying Spaniards intent on seizing it.[12] Pile might well have exercised concern, for a Spanish ship-of-war followed the *Virgin-*

ius out of Puerto Cabello, and only after a three-hour chase did the Cubans manage to elude their pursuer. At his next port Captain Smith listened to the friendly warning of the U.S. consul, "Why don't you get rid of that damned pirate? She is nothing but a pirate, and you will get caught by and by, and they will hang you."[13] Quesada soon was looking for a new captain.

After drydocking at Martinique the *Virginius* returned to Aspinwall early in 1873, to have its engines overhauled in preparation for another Cuban voyage, and it was here that it ran afoul of Lieutenant José Autran of the Spanish gunboat *Bazan* and had a close call with disaster. For three years the steamer had been gaining an unsavory reputation, and time and luck were beginning to run out. It was fortunate that two American gunboats, the *Canandaigua* and *Kansas*, the latter the ship that had escorted it to safety the previous year, rode at anchor.

Trouble this time began at a leisurely pace when Lieutenant Autran on June 3, 1873 sent word to Commander Allen V. Reed of the *Kansas*, the ranking American present, insisting that the *Virginius* was a pirate and subject to capture because it belonged to the Cuban rebels and had committed a hostile act against Spain by landing troops and arms in Cuba. Was the *Virginius*, he asked, entitled to fly the American flag? This might have been a rhetorical question, but Autran wanted a "definite answer." Commander Reed's reply was that the *Virginius* was an American vessel which he had every intention of protecting. Under the circumstances he could do nothing else, although he and most of the naval officers on the scene were skeptical of the *Virginius*'s claim to protection. Sensing Yankee defiance which could only assist the rebels, Autran responded that with all force at his command he would prevent the ship from sailing. The threat reached Quesada who announced he would sink his vessel rather than allow it to be captured.[14]

The two commanders, Spanish and American, had it within their power to bring their nations to hostilities. The Spanish commander seemed cool but willing to take drastic measures. Lieutenant Seaton Schroeder of the *Canandaigua,* four years out of Annapolis and with a fair knowledge of Spanish, was assigned to act as interpreter and had an opportunity to see the "opposition" at close quarters. He found the master of the *Bazan* a brave officer "who did his duty in a straightforward manner." Autran impressed the young man with the "unexcited exposition of his orders" in a dilemma that called for steady nerves.[15] The Spaniard made what seemed a reasonable request, that the *Virginius* go back to the United States so that the Spanish government might bring suit against it in court.[16] But when the United States consul in Aspinwall again came to the ship's defense, certifying that its papers were in order, Autran prepared to try desperate means to stop an enemy of his country. When on the afternoon of July 5, 1873, the oppressive tropic sun seemed to have encased all the ships in Aspinwall harbor, it was a surprise to the watch aboard the *Canandaigua* to see the bustling activity aboard the *Bazan*. Sighting his glasses on its deck he saw the two thirty-pound rifled cannon trained on the *Virginius*.

Again the *Virginius* got away. The men aboard the American ships were called to stations.[17] At 1:30 P.M. the *Virginius* got up steam, but did not attempt to move. At 2:30, Commander Reed moved the *Kansas* into position between the *Virginius* and the *Bazan*. There the ships lay for nearly four hours, each expecting treachery, until 6:10 when the *Virginius* slowly began to steam out of harbor while Commander Reed deftly kept his ship between pursuer and pursued.[18]

One can imagine the rage aboard the *Bazan* as a ship known to be carrying death to Spanish troops cleared Aspinwall harbor, but the *Bazan* could only stop the filibuster by firing through an American vessel. When Autran compared his orders and his two thirty-pounders against the yawning muzzles of two eleven-inch, four nine-inch, and two four-inch rifles aimed by the American warships, duty bowed to discretion.[19]

The *Kansas* escorted the *Virginius* well off the coast, against the possibility that Autran would change his mind and pursue. When satisfied, the American put about and returned. Black smoke billowing from its funnels, the *Virginius* could be seen shrinking into the horizon until night blended with smoke and the ship disappeared northeast toward Cuba.

(30)

If the *Bazan* had pursued, it would have overtaken the Cubans, for the *Virginius*'s speed was reduced by the weight of the large cargo, contraband from the New York Junta. After unloading the freight in Cuba it continued to Kingston, Jamaica, where the Cubans found plenty of sympathizers. There the steamer was to pick up another filibustering expedition.

Thomas H. Pearne, consul to Kingston, must have felt a novel responsibility when on July 9, 1873 the *Virginius* came into harbor. News of the escape from Aspinwall had spread, and would make the pages of the far-off New York newspapers. As it turned out, the *Virginius* was not prepared for further trouble. Most of the crew including the captain left soon after the steamer made Kingston. The vessel would be in port for some time, to make repairs and take on another crew, and over the next three months there was little movement around or aboard the vessel, other than that of an occasional workman.[20]

The *Virginius* lay idle at Kingston harbor until the arrival from New York in mid-October, 1873, of the American steamer *Atlas*. The consignee of Kingston, Altamont de Cordova, a Cuban sympathizer involved in aiding the revolutionists, wrote the customs agent, J. D. Young, for permission to have seven cases of goods assigned him from the *Atlas* transferred to the *Virginius* on payment of the duty. A rifle in one of the cases, Cordova assured the officials, "has been sent as a present to a gentleman who will leave in the *Virginius,* and I can't suppose that a man is not allowed to carry with him a single rifle. Then there are a few leggings and some cutlasses, these latter as you know are extensively used for agricultural purposes."[21] The British thought differently. "In view of the circumstances connected with the *Virginius*'s presence in these waters," the agent wrote, "I submit, for consideration, whether it is not tolerable certain that the remainder of the goods ticked off by Mr. de Cordova, are in fact 'munitions of war'."[22]

The *Atlas* had brought men as well as munitions. Local officials offered no resistance when about ninety-five men disembarked and went to the outskirts of Kingston where they drilled and waited for the expedition.[23]

(31)

GEORGE WASHINGTON RYAN.

JESUS DEL SOL.

BERNARE VARONA.

PEDRO CESPEDES

3. The soldier of fortune Ryan and his three Cuban comrades. From *Harper's Weekly*, November 29, 1873.

Officers and men destined to sail on the *Virginius* were composed of every type, from the selfless patriot dedicated to Cuba Libre to the purest adventurer. First on the roster was the commander-in-chief, General Bernabé Varona, called Bembetta. Although only twenty-eight years old, Bembetta had won distinction in virtually every engagement in the war, and alone among the Cubans on the *Atlas* he had risen to the rank of general. In a war marked by atrocities on both sides Bembetta was known for his insistence on humanity toward prisoners. He had spent the past year raising funds, and was rewarded by being made commander of the expedition.[24] His staff were Lieutenant Colonels Jesús del Sol and Agustin Santa Rosa. Del Sol had been a prosperous farmer before the war but had given up his lands to enter the service of the insurrection. Twice wounded in battle, he had escaped to the United States after being captured by the Spanish. Soon he boarded the *Atlas* to return to the war zone.[25] Santa Rosa, who traveled under the alias Francisco Rivera, had worked for Cuban independence since the López expedition of 1850. A fighter, he was devout in religion, and like a medieval knight never entered battle without praying for the souls of enemies he might slay. When he fell prisoner in 1871, his dual citizenship led to a successful effort by the United States to have him freed.[26] Now he too was returning to the fight. Finally, Pedro de Céspedes, younger brother of the President of the Cuban provisional government, signed on the *Virginius* to fight in Cuba. His name and position gave the little group of men a stamp of legitimacy, if any was needed.

The presence of these Cuban leaders aboard the *Virginius* would not have surprised anyone familiar with their backgrounds, but there were other men who in name and nationality seemed out of place. Among the individuals aboard the *Atlas* was a tall, clean-shaven young adventurer with the air of a swashbuckler who sported a broad hat and a vision of rich reward for his role in Cuban independence. If General William Ryan, known to newspapers in the United States as George Washington Ryan, showed the distant qualities of the dreamer, his life had been one of action. Born in 1840 in Ireland he had emigrated with his family to Canada.[27] Moving to the United States, he fought in the Civil War in a New York infantry regi-

(33)

4. Joseph Fry, the ill-fated captain of the *Virginius*. From *Harper's Weekly*, November 29, 1873.

ment, rising to the rank of lieutenant and winning a commendation for bravery in action. After Appomattox, he joined the ranks of restless men unprepared to return to peacetime pursuits and moved West to the mining camps of Montana. Back in New York by 1868, he became part of the Bohemian element of the city. Organization of the Cuban Junta that year brought opportunity for men with military experience like Ryan to take commissions, and he became a colonel with the self-breveted title of general.

If for Ryan and his Cuban companions of 1873 the forthcoming voyage was only one more incident in the five-year fight for Cuba Libre, for Captain Joseph Fry it was an adventure. Not that Fry was unfamiliar with risk. Born in Tampa, he had been a member of the second class to graduate from the Naval Academy, after which he had struggled with sea and wind for fifteen years until he resigned in February, 1861, to enter the Confederate navy and begin a four-year contest with the Federal Union.[28] In 1865, with no hope of resuming naval service and with the American merchant marine suffering a postwar depression, his circumstances began to deteriorate.[29] On arrival in Kingston, Captain Fry became the most important member of the expedition. His skill at navigation, rusty after years without practice, would enable the group to reach Cuba. Ryan and Bembetta could train the soldiers, but it would be wasted effort if they never closed with the enemy.

Fry had to round up a makeshift crew from unemployed seamen who might not be willing to sign if they knew the *Virginius*'s destination and business, but he recruited several men without difficulty. William Baynard, survivor of a recent shipwreck, was happy to join the crew as first mate for sixty dollars in gold per month with the understanding that the *Virginius* would engage in trade among the islands.[30] A native of Chester, England, Henry King had arrived in Jamaica as an oiler on the Liverpool steamer *Caribbean* and while in port contracted yellow fever and entered a hospital. When the master of a sailor's home found him a job as oiler on the *Virginius* he was in no position to turn it down. It was hardly a first-class job, but there were worse ships on the seas. The understanding was that the voyage would be only around the islands.[31] As for thirteen-year-old George Burke of Kingston, running away from home, the voyage was to be a lark. Falling in with a painter named South, he agreed to go with the man to Limon Bay aboard the *Virginius*, but South never showed up for the voyage. The boy paid the *Virginius*'s purser £2.10 for passage and was told he must work sweeping decks, helping the cook, and doing other odd jobs.[32] So too did sixteen-year-old Edward Scott of Salem, New Jersey sign aboard for adventure.[33]

While Fry was scouring Kingston for seamen, Ryan drilled the troops, saw the countryside, and attended "feast after feast and ball after ball" given by Cuban sympathizers for officers of the expedition. The Peruvian minister gave the first dance in honor of Generals Bembetta and Ryan. De Cordova and other prominent Jamaicans followed this example. The wealth and fashion of Kingston presented itself at the functions. In an age before technological warfare, an officer's competence in the ballroom was scarcely less important than bravery on the battlefield, and Ryan ably filled both roles. He wrote George W. Crook, of later Indian war fame, that "The place is filled with beautiful women, and gay and splendid fellows, generous to a fault and liberal as princes; must say that I never received such attention. I regret that want of time will prevent giving you a detailed account of my adventures. I am as fat as a bull and gay as a lark and leave this place with many regrets."[34]

The hour of departure had come, for in his letter to Crook, dated October 23, 1873, Ryan remarked that "in one hour we leave for Cuba. This is quite unexpected, as we did not expect to go until to-morrow."[35] A great party of sympathizers boarded the steamer to sail to the edge of the harbor. It must have been a gala occasion, certainly one on which hope rested. The *Virginius* was carrying a group which was to converge with other bands of patriots. Ryan's friend Major J.C. Harris of Virginia had written, "Much depends upon the success of this expedition, and the combination aboard. We take only 300 men from this port, but we will be joined by two other parties and I am confident of success."[36]

The ship picked up steam, and the insurgents bade good-bye to their well-wishers. A group of young Cuban stowaways was discovered at the final moment and placed in the last launch to go ashore.

Fry set a course for Jeremie on the island of Haiti. The *Virginius* enjoyed good weather and calm seas, reaching port on the twenty-fifth. There it signaled a schooner in the inter-island trade to stop. When the schooner sailed on, Bembetta ordered four men with revolvers into a boat to seize the craft. The deed accomplished, the schooner's captain was put aboard the *Virginius* to pilot the ship into Jeremie where the group remained a day before the authorities ordered them out.[37]

The next port of call was Port-au-Prince, arriving at ten o'clock in the morning, and that night two boats put alongside and transferred three hundred Remingtons, 300,000 cartridges, and a man in charge of the weapons.[38] Some men now wanted out, and Evaristo Sanchez Sunsunegeri was one of them. Eighteen years old, he had left his native Havana supposedly for employment in the United States, but within a month was aboard the *Atlas* bound for Cuba. He and two other individuals asked to leave. When the three men came to his cabin Bembetta showed determination to see the expedition through. Too much had been expended, he told them. What assurance was there that they would not go straight to the Spanish? If they persisted in their request, Bembetta left no doubt they would not leave the ship alive.[39]

Haitian officials permitted the *Virginius* to load without interference. The next morning the Spanish minister protested to no avail for within the hour the ship stood out to sea.[40]

From Port-au-Prince the *Virginius* went to Comito, where Bembetta disembarked and returned with eight hundred daggers, eight hundred machetes, a barrel of powder, and a case of shoes. Each man received a dagger and shoes. Rifles were not yet distributed but tied in parcels of ten and placed in the ship's armory. Cartridges were in bags, which were put in cases. The expedition left Comito the same day, for Bembetta wished to go to Puerto Simones where two field guns were buried. Ryan opposed this course as taking too much time because the ship was leaking. The vessel's crowded condition also would lead to trouble among the men. The steamer headed for Cuba where no landing spot had been selected. From Bembetta's group a sergeant, two corporals,

(37)

and fourteen men were chosen to explore the land armed with machetes and carbines.[41] The scouts never reached shore. About six miles from land, with the prow pointed toward Cuba and the bluish-green hills of Guantánamo visible through the mist, the men of the *Virginius* beheld the *Tornado*.

CHAPTER FOUR

Death to Rebels

THE Spanish corvette *Tornado* had had a checkered career, like the *Virginius*. Indeed it had been constructed in 1864 in the very same Scottish shipyard. Likewise designated for the Confederacy, it had not reached the South, and eventually was sold to the Peruvian government, which then sold it to Spain. Under Captain Dionisio Costilla it sailed from Santiago on October 29, 1873, and after cruising under steam during the night along the coast put out to sea as morning broke. Under order to patrol against blockade-runners, Costilla was watchful for the *Virginius* which reports said had cleared Kingston a week before. He knew a rebel ship would risk landing only during darkness, and during daylight would reduce steam and stand off the coast to avoid being seen.[1]

At about ten o'clock on the morning of October 30 the watch reported a schooner headed toward Jamaica and the *Tornado* gave chase. This ship turned out to be an American vessel, the *Village Belle,* one day out of Santiago bound for Jamaica. It came to a halt and received a boarding party.[2] After one hour the *Tornado* waved the American ship on, then reduced speed to conserve coal and sailed along the coast for eighteen miles. At half past two that afternoon the smoke of a steamer appeared on the horizon to the southwest. Gradually the ship drew nearer, one point to the east of the Spaniard. Costilla ordered his boilers fired. Suddenly the stranger shifted course to south southwest. From course and the steamer's outline Costilla believed it to be the *Virginius.* Obviously coming from Jamaica, its course was not what a ship would have held in the inter-island trade. As the steamer changed direction the Spaniards could see its boilers firing up.[3]

That same afternoon, while Guantánamo still was in sight, the crew of the *Village Belle* again encountered the *Tornado,*

(39)

and several miles in front a long black two-masted steamer, low in the water, heading for Kingston streaming black smoke. Three miles to stern the *Tornado* drew steadily closer. As the fleeing vessel passed within a short distance of the *Belle* the latter ship's crew could see individuals on deck and made out the name *Virginius*. Well before the sun began to set, the *Tornado* was close enough to recognize two stacks and two masts which increased Costilla's suspicion that the fugitive was "The pirate *Virginius*."[4]

To Joseph Fry, sight of the *Tornado* must have been the final blow. For a week the *Virginius* had limped from one port to another, engines constantly in danger of breaking down in spite of the efforts of engineers Henry King and Henry Knight. With some of the would-be guerrillas having undergone changes of heart, the crew had shown signs of re-belling until Bembetta threatened to kill anyone who asked out. With a Spanish corvette closing in, Fry might well have thought he should have remained, even in poverty, with his family in New Orleans.

Although beyond gun range, the *Tornado* fired. The men of the *Virginius* saw a cloud of white smoke and heard the dull boom. Fry hoped to maintain course until darkness.

"If we can hang him up until nightfall," he told Bembetta, "I think I shall be able to get away."

Turning to Knight, Fry asked, "Can't you give her more steam?"

Knight promised the "top notch" but said the boilers might explode.

Replied Fry, "Let her go for all she is worth."[5]

After a few minutes the pressure began to build, and the ship's creaking and shaking seemed to increase ten-fold. The *Virginius* was like a prey fleeing a huntsman. In the engine room firemen anxiously watched the boiler pressure, dread-ing what might happen. They began feeding some hams from the ship's larder. Bembetta ordered other supplies thrown overboard. It would do the Cuban cause no good if excess weight caused the ship to be captured.[6]

Five o'clock became six o'clock; six turned to seven. The shadows of the *Virginius* became longer on the waves. Dark-ness was beginning. Aboard the Spaniard the prayers were

(40)

for light to keep the outline two miles ahead of them in sight. To the joy of the pursuer and anguish of the pursued, a bright moon now came out, giving light for the drama below.

The outcome of the chase was being decided in the engine room of the *Virginius*. The machines' convulsions were beginning to loosen the ship's caulking, and leaks were appearing. The *Virginius* was taking water too rapidly for the pumps. Speed fell from twelve knots to seven, distance between the two ships narrowed. To Bembetta, pacing the deck, the hours seemed endless. Already his crew had pushed into the sea material meant for comrades in the Sierra Madre Oriente. Guns and equipment enough to keep a guerrilla army in the field for six months were beyond recovery. He was silently weighing the chances for escape when Fry came to end his hopes. Even in the moonlight one could see that Fry was pale.

"I am afraid we will have to give up," Fry told him. "The shaking of the ship has loosed the caulking and we are sinking badly."[7]

Bembetta, Fry, and Ryan held a council of war. At that moment the *Tornado* fired a second shot. The big ball skimmed over the seas, dropping four cable lengths (approximately one-half mile) to starboard. A third shot did no more damage, but a fourth struck so close to the rigging that the men ducked apprehensively. Bembetta considered blowing up the vessel but decided against it. Then a fifth shot smashed into the steamer's stack, putting an end to further debate.[8]

"The jig is up!" Fry cried. "Round her to and stop the engines."

The last chance of the *Virginius,* as all the men believed, lay in claiming protection of the American flag that still flew from the mast.[9]

Aboard the *Tornado* jubilation reigned. The chase had ended. Now came the task of boarding and securing the prize. Sailors tumbled over one another to have the honor. Under command of two ensigns, Don Ruiz Pardo and Don Angel Ortiz Monasterio, two boats pushed off. Crews, made up of all ranks, pulled with a will, and under the bright moon drew closer to the black shape lying silent and motionless in

(41)

the water ahead. Angel Ortiz reached the *Virginius* first. It must have been a nervous moment for the young officer who could not be sure if the opponents would surrender or fire at them. Hailing the steamer he shouted that force would be met with force.[10] Followed by his men he climbed aboard, the only noise coming from the triumphant Spanish seamen. Ortiz ordered his men to take charge of the engine room, at the same time announcing that presence of Spaniards aboard would not stop the *Tornado* from sinking the ship if it offered resistance. At that moment Ruiz Pardo's boat arrived, which ended any hope of Bembetta or the others of overcoming their captors.

Even as Spanish seamen took possession of the deck, the *Virginius*'s crew was throwing cargo out the portholes and over the prow. Leading a party below deck, Ortiz found a group of men huddled in the forecastle and ordered them up to the quarter-deck. Search of the cabins showed wild disorder with trunks open, clothes strewn about, boxes of car-

5. Artist's conception of the capture. From *Harper's Weekly*, November 29, 1873.

tridges open, machetes, insurgent cockades, saddles, and paper scattered about.[11] Quick examination of the engines revealed the machinery and packing in bad shape. The ship was taking water through a poorly caulked point toward the prow and below the water line.

The Spaniards ordered the American flag down, which Ortiz believed, "as a pirate, the ship should not be permitted to use."[12] One of the crewmen, the sixteen-year-old Edward Scott, shouted back, "Take it down yourselves." They did. Sailors tore the flag from its mast and raised the red and yellow banner of Spain. As the American standard came down, Spanish officers grabbed it and threw it to the deck. The flag lay where it dropped, with busy Spaniards trampling over it to carry on their duties. Some came forward to spit on the flag that for five years had sheltered so many of Spain's enemies. As one man so displayed his contempt, Ryan quietly remarked to fellow prisoners what must have been the thoughts of many, "That means war, boys, if we ever get out of this."[13]

Within half an hour the Spaniards had stripped, searched, and bound the prisoners, while Ryan sneered so openly, that his friends expected him to be killed on the spot. To the *Tornado* they transferred all but Fry and the engineer King. Guards aboard the corvette handled the prisoners roughly; for several hours none was fed. Finally they received brandy, cheese and crackers. While they waited the *Tornado* was slowly taking the *Virginius* in tow, and with a crew of jubilant Spaniards, and the dejected, fearful Cubans, began the voyage back to Santiago and Spanish justice.

At 2:00 A.M., November 1, night watch on the deck of the *Village Belle* saw the result of the chase. The black outlines of two ships, the *Tornado* in front and the *Virginius* behind, passing in the night, headed toward Santiago.[14]

That first day of November, 1873, the *Virginius* was to lie quietly in Santiago harbor with the American flag still conspicuously on its quarter deck, trampled by the crew. Not until next evening was the flag removed. No public celebration occurred. Other than pealing of bells there was nothing to indicate a triumph. One American noted that things seemed excessively quiet, as though the whole city awaited some great event.[15]

As the prisoners went ashore from the *Tornado* next after-noon, silent throngs crowded the windows and roof tops to see what was to have been a liberating group marched to jail. All the men except Ryan, Bembetta, del Sol and Céspedes had elbows pinned behind, hands tied in front. The four leaders remained apart as the men formed columns and marched away under guard from the waterfront toward the city jail.[16]

The only protection the flag could now give had to come through efforts of Emil G. Schmitt, American vice consul in Santiago, since Arthur W. Young, the consul, was in the United States and not expected back for several weeks. After a century the few surviving records do little more than outline Schmitt's career. He had been appointed vice consul for Santiago in July, 1871. He belonged to a branch of government totally at the disposal of domestic politicians. Often the best representatives were men like the consul general in Havana, Henry C. Hall, who had been in business in the country before becoming part of the consular service.

The best trained, most experienced consul would have been extended in the circumstances in which Schmitt now found himself.[17] Anxious to know the condition of the men he went to the jail, but authorities denied him permission to see the prisoners. As he knew, the plight of the captives would be covered by the treaty between the United States and Spain which still governed relations, the well-known Treaty of 1795, negotiated and signed by Thomas Pinckney at San Lorenzo. Article VII of that document agreed that citizens of both countries "shall be allowed to employ such Advocates, Sollicitors [sic], Notaries, Agents, and Factors as they may judge proper . . . in all their trials at law in which they may be concerned."[18] The prisoners, whom Schmitt understood to be Americans, were entitled to see the consul and have legal aid. Even so, he realized that if the *Virginius* was flying the American flag illegally the men had forfeited their right to protection. The first thing to do was to wire Kingston to find out the ship's status. Until then he would proceed under assumption that the ship was American.[19]

Schmitt went to the office of the Cuba Submarine Cable

Company to wire Kingston. It was impossible to reach Consul General Hall in Havana because either a storm or insurgents had cut the wire to the Cuban capital. The only link with the outside world was the cable to Jamaica. But Schmitt found his message could not be sent owing to an order by the military commander of Santiago, General Don Juan N. Burriel. Furious at this obstruction he protested to the company agent, who was helpless for "according to the concession to the company, the government has an absolute right to censure, and of impeding and preventing the sending of such messages as it objects to."[20]

No help would be received by telegraph. General Burriel offered the sole hope, and rumor now circulated that Burriel planned to take responsibility for immediate executions before foreign countries could intervene on behalf of the prisoners.[21] Schmitt wrote the general on the day after the *Virginius* arrived. His letter went unanswered. Next morning he tried again; no answer. At half-past six that evening, November 3, he again wrote Burriel and "solemnly" protested the conduct of the Spanish government.[22]

Even as he wrote, the Spanish were trying the prisoners. The previous night a court martial had convened. It operated quickly, for Ryan and the three Cubans, Bembetta, Quesada, and del Sol, had been tried in absentia earlier in the uprising and sentenced to death. According to military law all that was necessary was to identify them and carry out the sentence. Although the United States government had protested this rule and Spain gave assurance it would be suspended, the decree was still being enforced. With guards being reinforced and a great deal of troop movement in and around the prison, the prospects of the captives were ominous.[23]

Schmitt determined to see Burriel. The meeting proved disappointing. It had been a tiring day, the general said. He would have answered the consul's letters sooner but had not come to his office as he had been engaged "in the meditation of the divine mysteries of All Saints, and the commemoration of All Souls Day."[24]

Schmitt faced up to the general, and what had begun as a strained conversation became more so. Burriel's chief of staff came into the room and said Ryan was an Englishman and

(45)

Schmitt had been so informed. Burriel accused Schmitt of concealing the information. When Schmitt assured him that Ryan was a naturalized citizen, Burriel exploded until it seemed the general's shouts could be heard a block away. He accused Schmitt of treachery. Struggling for control, the consul reminded Burriel that he was a representative of the United States and expected to be so treated.[25] Burriel lowered his voice, but it was plain he considered Schmitt another Yankee against the Spanish government. The two men drew off. Schmitt went back to his quarters where he summed up his feeling about his encounter in a dispatch to Hall, "All Soul's Day, fine day to kill a man!"[26]

Early in the morning of November 4 a guard detachment formed in front of the Santiago jail. For Ryan it must have been a long night. Repeated efforts to talk to the British consul, whom he had asked for instead of Schmitt, had failed. He had written letters to friends and to his fiancée in New York and composed a will, but there was no guarantee any of these missives would find their way into the hands for which they were intended. All that remained was to prepare for death, an appointment he had managed to elude since joining the Union army over a decade before. But he was ready. Proud of his appearance to the end, he dressed in a blue vest over a white shirt with the single silver star of a brigadier general in the insurrectionary army pinned over his left breast.[27]

At a quarter to seven that morning, together with Bembetta, del Sol and Céspedes, he walked out of jail. Ryan waved away a priest who offered last rites, lit a cigar, set his sombrero at a jaunty angle, and fell in with his companions. A drummer began to beat the death march, and the little column surrounded by guards moved forward. Ryan called out to the other prisoners, "I guess it is death this time. Goodby boys and good luck."[28] It was about a ten-minute walk. Ryan continued to puff his cigar and trudged along. A crowd had gathered along the line of march. One spectator remembered that he "showed more grit and courage than one would have thought possible."[29]

At the end of the street down which they passed there came into view a long square structure with whitewashed walls between ten and twenty feet high mounted by a roof of dark tiles with projecting eaves. It was a former slaughterhouse, used by the Spanish army's squads since the insurrection. At the foot of the wall was a ditch two feet deep to catch rain. Along one wall the light-colored soil had taken on a darker tinge. When the party arrived at the wall the drumming ceased. Spectators, mostly silent, formed on three sides.[30] The only sound was commands of an officer as the firing squad stepped forward. A soldier pushed Bembetta and del Sol forward first. Kneeling with their faces to the wall, the two men kept their courage to the end. The firing squad poured a volley into their backs. Ryan and Céspedes stood through the shooting, Ryan puffing his cigar. Then it was their turn. They protested bitterly against kneeling for death. There was a scuffle as the executioners forced them to the ground, but allowed them to face the squad. At the last moment, before the firing, Ryan flung away his cigar.[31]

That same day Burriel sent a dispatch to Captain General Juan Jovellar in Havana telling of the execution of four patriot generals: Bernabe Varona, alias Bembetta, General of Division; Pedro Céspedes, Commanding General of Cienfuegos; General Jesús del Sol; and Brigadier General George Washington Ryan. The executions, he wrote, "took place in the presence of the entire corps of Volunteers, the force of regular infantry and the sailors from the fleet. An immense concourse of people also witnessed the act. The best order prevailed. The prisoners met their death with composure."[32]

British Acting Vice Consul Theodore Brooks had been an interested spectator on Saturday, November 1, when the local people had flocked to the waterfront to see the *Tornado* and its captive ship, and although Brooks thought there might be some British subjects among the prisoners, he believed, given the reputation of the *Virginius* and the American flag flying from the vessel captured, that any British subject should look for help to the American consul. He had confined himself to keeping informed of what was happening to the crew.[33]

On Sunday, Brooks began to hear news of Burriel's refusal to allow Schmitt to wire Jamaica, and of a division of prisoners by the military and naval authorities, the former holding the soldiers of the expedition and the latter taking the crew.

During the following days he learned of Schmitt's argument with Burriel and of Ryan proclaiming himself a British subject.[34]

Thursday, the sixth, Brooks discovered that a naval court martial was going to condemn thirty-seven of the crew. Certain there would be Britishers among them he now went to the telegraph office. Without obstruction Brooks wired Jamaica, and he soon received a reply from the governor telling him to make every effort to save any innocent British subject.[35] This was not what Brooks intended, and it furnished little ammunition to deal with Burriel, but later that afternoon he received the telegram he was looking for, in the form of a message from Commodore A. F. R. de Horsey of the Royal Navy who told him to protest in his name against execution of any British subject.[36]

Interestedly, it was not a message from Brooks that caused the commodore to champion the unfortunate filibusterers; that honor belonged to Altamont de Cordova, consignee of the *Virginius* in Kingston. News of the capture had circulated, and de Cordova had shared the Cuban community's despair, but unlike the Cubans he had determined to do something to prevent a massacre of the men. Going to the head of the telegraph office in Kingston he managed to get the office opened around the clock and sent a message to Santiago instructing the office there to remain open until the Kingston office told them they might close. He then saw the local American consul and had him forward a message to the U.S.S. *Wyoming* in Aspinwall, ordering its commander to start for Santiago immediately.[37]

Nothing if not active, de Cordova took a boat from Kingston across the bay to the naval station at Port Royal and went to see Commodore de Horsey.[38]

"I don't see what I can do in the matter," de Horsey declared. "It is now five o'clock, and the telegraph office closes at that hour. Even if I wanted to send a message I have no opportunity to do so."

The consignee explained he had arranged for offices to remain open all night.

The commodore wavered. "I hardly see what I can do, Mr. de Cordova. What is it you ask?"

(48)

De Cordova entreated him to protest further executions and send a ship to Santiago.

"I have only one vessel in the harbor, and I must keep her for an emergency."

"The emergency has arisen," declared de Cordova.

Her Majesty's Commander of West Indian Naval Forces was trapped. Excusing himself to see what he could do, he gave orders to prepare for sea to the captain of H.M.S. *Niobe,* Sir Lambton Lorraine. At the same time he sent the message to Brooks to protest in his name the executions.[39]

For the era of gunboat diplomacy the captain of the *Niobe* was a suitable man for what promised to be a gallant dash to rescue British subjects. A few months previously Lorraine had been responsible for bombardment of a Nicaraguan town which somehow had been guilty of insufficient protection of British subjects. He was an old sea dog of stocky build, with a thick, short neck which gave the look of an overweight boxer. His chin, covered by a stubble of beard, added to the fighting appearance. When he received de Horsey's orders he lost no time, putting out so quickly he left some of his crew on the dock watching the ship as it went to sea.[40]

Back in Santiago, Theodore Brooks now armed with imperial authority went to call on Burriel and advanced the commodore's request for a delay of execution without mentioning the protest. The governor denied the request because he was under superior orders, he said, and could "in no way intervene in the action of the law."[41] Although Burriel was polite his manner gave the impression that he found the subject disagreeable. Brooks should see the captain of the port, the general said.[42] The British acting vice consul now took his case to the captain of the port to whom he voiced a similar appeal. He received the same answer. The matter was out of his hands, but the captain promised to send notes on the sixteen British subjects condemned to death by court martial the previous night. With his hope of a stay of execution exhausted, Brooks played his last card and addressed a message to Burriel in which he protested in Commodore de Horsey's name. Time was running short. Four o'clock was the hour for additional executions. As the afternoon sped on, Brooks received a cable from Governor Sir John P. Grant to

6. Sir Lambton Lorraine, whose timely arrival halted executions. From *Harper's Weekly*, November 29, 1873.

make an urgent appeal. He returned to Burriel to deliver the appeal but got less satisfaction than before. The general turned him down curtly. The only hope for the men lay with the *Niobe* now steaming across the Caribbean from Port Royal.[43]

In the city jail, Captain Fry and thirty-six men were facing their last hours on earth. The night before, they had been tried before naval authorities. Ironically the court prosecutor or fiscal was Lieutenant José Maria Autran, commander of the *Bazan,* who earlier had seen the *Virginius* slip through his fingers. The lieutenant was known as a man who favored harsh punishment for gunrunners and once had said that the Spanish navy should shoot every foreign crew "found anywhere near the Cuban coast." The filibusters were tried under Captain General Dulce's 1869 decree, that all vessels captured on the high seas near Cuba with men and munitions should be treated as pirates and their crews immediately executed.[44]

Interrogation had brought Fry out in strong defense of his men:

> With permission of the consul, I wish to say a few words in favor of the crew of the *Virginius,* and the mitigation of their punishment. The pilot had just escaped from a shipwreck, and needed an advance of salary to buy clothes and have them made. The man Briton was my servant, hired by the day, when we were in port, and not inscribed on the roll. He is almost an idiot and ought not to suffer.[45]

He stoutly denied knowledge of the law of 1869. If he had not heard of the act then his men could not have. "I was continually in the company of people who ought to have known of it, and not one alluded to the fact. In a word, I believe that it is not known, and that the world will be painfully surprised at learning the sacrifice of lives."[46] Writing to a friend before the trial, Fry expressed few doubts of the verdict.

> I have been captured by the *Tornado,* subjected to a rigid examination and cross-examination, and tonight have been told officially that tomorrow morning I and thirty others will be tried by court martial. They did not add "and shot"

(51)

but I look upon it as a polite way of making that announcement.[47]

After the trial Fry was locked with his crew in a large, bare room. At eight o'clock on the morning of November 7 the same officer and squad of soldiers who had led Ryan and companions to death appeared. One by one, thirty-seven names were called. Fry's was first. As each man stepped to the front a mournful chorus of *adios* came from all sides. The sentence was to have been carried out the next day, November 8, but apparently Burriel had heard of departure of the *Niobe* and had advanced the date. The men marched down a long hall to a chapel for preparation of their souls for eternity. As the priest intoned, some men rested their heads on their hands, some knelt, some sat gazing at the priest as though they scarcely comprehended.[48]

The French consul in Santiago, Alphonse Garrus, and his *chancelier* joined Schmitt in the U.S. consulate, a few doors from the jail, to watch the prisoners pass on their way. As the men went into the street, four men were told to step aside. These prisoners were reprieved for the moment. The guards were furious and with blows and curses moved the four men slowly back toward the prison by way of the execution wall. The remaining prisoners then marched past the consular office in ranks of four by four. Some saluted the bare flagstaff of the consulate by inclining their heads. The last to go by were Captain Fry and two other men who besides saluting waved a mournful goodby to Schmitt and the Frenchmen standing on the consulate's piazza.[49]

When the men reached the wall, the firing squad was resting arms in a long line. A sergeant wasted no time running among the prisoners pushing each man by his shoulders against the wall. Fry was the only man not bound. Charles Bell, mate of the American ship *Morning Star* docked in the harbor, witnessed the scene. Coming forward he gave Fry a drink of water. Fry repeated his story that he had never heard of the act under which he was to be shot. Bell hurried away from the wall. The crew knelt and in an emotional scene Fry went down the line saying goodbye. When he reached the end he took off his cap and seemed to be offering a prayer which was punctuated by commands from the firing squad officer. A ragged volley flashed toward the men. Fry fell forward, dead at the first fire. Others were still standing, leaning against the wall. Some bent forward. Many were on the ground in agony. Poor marksmanship and nervousness had made a butcher's job. Some of the squad rushed forward to administer the *coup de grâce* and shoved muskets into the men's mouths. Shooting continued for five minutes until thirty-seven men lay dead in heaps before the wall. To American sailors in Santiago harbor it sounded like fireworks on the Fourth of July. A wagon drove up, the bodies were piled on hastily, and it drove off.[50]

While the crew had languished in prison and Schmitt had struggled with Burriel's obstinacy, the only other American in a position to help had been Robert Nunes of the Kingston consulate. Nunes was of cautious mind. When Schmitt had inquired about the nationality of the *Virginius*, Nunes cabled it was American and then turned to other issues.[51] At 8:00 A.M. on the day of the execution of Fry and his men, Nunes received a note from British Colonial Secretary William S. Young telling him that Governor Grant believed the *Virginius* was not a pirate and any shooting of British subjects illegal.[52] News that the *Niobe* had sailed galvanized Nunes, who telegraphed the *Wyoming* at Aspinwall that "American lives might require protection."[53] With receipt of more news from Santiago next day, Nunes wrote more urgently. Captain William Cushing, no doubt more dubious of the *Virginius*'s right to protection by virtue of his acquaintance with its past, cabled back on November 8 for "more facts."[54] Nunes recounted the capture in neutral waters and the shooting of Americans. His telegram was followed by one from Schmitt telling Cushing of Ryan's and Fry's execution and that there was "no American war vessel about."[55] The implication was that Cushing should not lose time. But Schmitt's telegram reached Kingston on Sunday, and it was Monday before the message was relayed. November 10, nearly two weeks after capture of the *Virginius,* a week after Ryan's death, Cushing began to coal for the voyage. He reached Jamaica where he coaled again on the fourteenth and departed for Cuba the next morning.

(53)

Meanwhile the prison doors had opened and closed for the last time on twelve more men.[56] By now Burriel's vengeance was beginning to repel even those who opposed the insurrection. After the morning's High Mass, several ladies had stopped at the prison door, knelt, and offered prayers for those in jail and for the souls of the departed. About ten o'clock that morning, charitable societies headed by the clergy went to the general and asked that the bloodshed halt.[57] Their request was to be granted but not because of any mercy on Burriel's part, for at 1:00 P.M. Sir Lambton Lorraine's *Niobe* dropped anchor in Santiago harbor.[58]

The twelve men shot shortly before the *Niobe*'s arrival would be the last. Lorraine and Brooks were ushered into General Burriel's office where they lodged a more formidable protest. The governor now greeted his visitors politely. In response to Lorraine's request concerning British prisoners he again gave his answer, that he had his duty under law, that superior orders (Burriel had no superior in the Santiago district) left no choice. But his work was accomplished, the leaders of the expedition in their graves, and he knew resistance now was accompanied by the force necessary to halt his plans. The Royal Navy could not be taken lightly. Burriel told the Englishmen he was "open to petitions but not demands." He could give assurance that no more prisoners would be shot that day.[59]

7. H.M.S. *Niobe* at anchor in Santiago Harbor. From *Harper's Weekly*, November 29, 1873.

CHAPTER FIVE

A Nation's Righteous Anger

ON Monday evening, November 3, 1873, Secretary of State and Mrs. Hamilton Fish, accompanied by Secretary of the Navy George M. Robeson and General William T. Sherman, attended a production at Wall's Opera House of Bulwer Lyton's drama "Cardinal Richelieu," by invitation of the management.[1] Fish had been away from Washington for a month, but now prepared to involve himself—among other activities—in the round of charges, denials, and evasions that had marked American diplomacy with Spain for nearly five years.

Two days later, Wednesday night, November 5, word of capture of the *Virginius* came into the Department from Consul General Hall in Havana.[2] The message reported that a tribunal would try the men as pirates.[3] The next day the secretary accompanied President Grant to a fair in Alexandria, returning late in the afternoon. An aide handed him a dispatch from General Sickles in Madrid reporting the capture and Sickles's request that word be sent the captain general in Cuba "to await orders from this government [Madrid] before inflicting penalties on passengers or crew."[4]

Grant customarily held Cabinet meetings on Tuesdays and Fridays, and at the session of Friday, November 7, Cuba appeared as the first order of business. The *Virginius* was of course a familiar name to Fish, for his diary and papers were full of Spanish complaints about the ship. There seemed no reason to worry more about its capture than about other seizures by Spain since 1868. At the meeting Grant signed a commission for Hall to become a permanent consul general. Then Fish related the information he possessed on capture of the *Virginius*.[5]

During the discussion Fish received a telegram date-line Havana, marked urgent, sent by A. L. Cobright of the Associated Press. It was the first news of the deaths of Ryan and companions on November 4. A colloquy followed on legal responsibilities for the capture and shootings, and Grant passed to Fish a note containing a question he had just written: "Would it not be well to telegraph to Sickles that the summary infliction of the death penalty upon the prisoners . . .will necessarily attract much attention in this country, and will be regarded as an inhuman act not in accordance with the spirit of the civilization of the nineteenth century?"[6] Grant's suggestion was approved. The Cabinet then forgot foreign affairs and turned to domestic financial matters.[7] The new incident would provide arguments for persons who wanted intervention, but there was no reason it could not be tolerated as others had been.

Saturday, November 8, Fish had regular appointments with the diplomatic corps and the first conference was with the Spanish minister, Don José Polo de Barnabé. Polo had spent his life in the Spanish navy rather than the legations and embassies of Europe. He had become one of Spain's leading officers, holding commands in the wars in Latin America during the 1860s. Fluent in English and a devout Republican, he had been the choice of the Spanish government as minister to Washington to succeed López Roberts in 1872. As aristocratic in bearing as Fish, he made up in character what he lacked in experience. Much, one might venture in retrospect, is beyond the reach of routine diplomacy. Nations whose interests are in conflict will seldom find their differences amenable even to the best diplomacy. But there are times when men of similar personality who speak frankly but with respect can smooth differences which more skilled men might turn into major problems. Two such men were Fish and Polo de Barnabé.

Polo presented two new members of his legation, who then withdrew, leaving himself and Fish to conduct their nations' business. The secretary brought up the *Virginius*. Polo disclaimed knowledge of the incident beyond what he had read in the newspapers but asked if Fish knew whether the ship was captured in British waters. The American referred to a story in Madrid papers of an official announcement that seizure had occurred six miles from Jamaica. Fish would not admit the right of capture beyond the three-mile limit, particularly since he believed the ship to have been flying the flag of the United States which should have given it immunity as a neutral vessel. Polo asked Fish confidentially if he would furnish evidence that the ship was flying the Stars and Stripes. With their positions as clear as scanty information enabled them to be, Polo withdrew.[8]

Interest in the incident was demonstrated by Fish's subsequent interview with Sir Edward Thornton, a tall lean figure, clean shaven, one of Secretary Fish's friends in Washington. Like Polo, Thornton was a man whom Fish could respect and with whom he could converse freely.[9] The Englishman asked information of the *Virginius*'s position at the time of capture. Fish repeated the Madrid *Gazette*'s statement that the ship was six miles from Jamaica which would place it in international waters, and added it was flying the American flag. Sir Edward hoped the information was correct but believed there would be conflicting evidence.[10] He mentioned he had spoken to Polo that morning and announced his government's condemnation of the executions. He feared the executions would strengthen Fish's enemies in Congress and reopen the question of belligerency.[11] He gave no hint of Britain's position, leaving Fish to wonder if there might soon be three parties in Cuba's civil war.[12]

At their next meeting on Tuesday, November 11, the Cabinet discussed intervention in Cuba. After a long debate the Cabinet concluded that war was not desirable although it might be "within the contingencies."[13] Someone asked, why not recognize a state of belligerency? It was an old question, but Fish justified nonrecognition on the ground that the rebels lacked sufficient power. He did recommend the strongest measure he had espoused since the beginning of the rebellion, an embargo on trade. To balance that he urged expressions of "kindness and sympathy" to the Republican government in Madrid.[14]

Perhaps Fish was apprehensive, for he questioned Secretary Robeson about the preparedness of the navy. The reply was that the ships were generally in good condition and several monitors could go to sea on short notice. Grant told Robeson to send a vessel to Santiago.[15] The next day Robeson called to report that the *Kansas* was about ready to sail.

(59)

Until now, November 12, the problem in Santiago had looked like a nuisance, but no sooner had Robeson left than Fish received a telegram from Hall in Havana with the stunning news of the execution of Captain Fry and thirty-six crew members. The question of the *Virginius* had to be reexamined. The secretary sent the telegram to Grant and took a carriage to the Navy Department. A copy of the cable went to the commander of the *Kansas* which was to sail from New York the next day.[16]

The secretary fired off an angry cable to Sickles. He was telegraphing for more information, he told the minister, and "if the report be confirmed" ordered Sickles to "protest in the name of this government and of civilization and humanity. . . and declare that this government will demand the most ample reparation of any wrong which may have been committed upon any of its citizens or upon its flag." He admitted "grave suspicions" concerning the right of the *Virginius* to carry the American flag.[17]

Fish met Polo on November 13 and launched into a series of protests that dramatized his anger. He objected both to the executions and Burriel's refusal to allow Schmitt to cable Kingston. The governor general had refused to allow Consul General Hall to represent the case and insisted that "everything should go through the regular diplomatic channels at Madrid."[18] Like most Americans Fish was sympathetic toward the Spanish republic but not toward the policies of Spain in Cuba. The best hope for avoiding war, he said, lay in Spain's convincing the Cubans that because of civil war in Spain the Madrid government could no longer protect foreigners in Cuba and it was up to other nations to seek their own remedies on the island. The way to clear the situation, Fish said confidentially, although he would not say so to leaders in Madrid, was for Spain to give the United States a free hand in dealing with the Cuban incident.[19]

Unfortunately Fish did not record the minister's reply, but Polo surely realized that the patience of Fish could be exhausted. He must have reported the secretary's "unofficial" remark in Madrid. The *Virginius* affair appeared to be the excuse the Yankees had needed for years to seize the island. If Spain turned the island over to American troops, even if remaining nominally the island's owner, it would be equivalent to giving the Americans a bill of sale with only the date left to be filled in.

Polo's apprehension would have been roused even more if he could have heard the conversation between Fish and the secretary's next visitor, Edwards Villeva, the Peruvian chargé d'affaires. Relations had strained between Peru and Spain, and like the citizens of many former colonies Peruvians missed no opportunity to insult the former masters. Villeva's government had recognized both the belligerency and independence of the Cuban rebels, and he unhesitatingly promised that should war break out Peru would join the United States. In view of suggestions by other Latin American nations it is doubtful that the offer surprised the secretary. Fish gave no assurance but encouraged the chargé to believe he would communicate if the administration decided to act.[20]

At the Friday Cabinet meeting, November 14, the topic once again was the *Virginius*. During the discussion a note was handed in from W. H. Clark of the American Press Association that Santiago authorities had shot one hundred and eleven more passengers! Before the meeting Fish had drafted a cable to Sickles to make demands and if they were not met to close the legation. Now the message seemed right. Grant approved. Postmaster General Creswell demurred, explaining he wished for "something more prompt and decided." When asked to elaborate, he said he could not, "but feared that Spain would comply with the requisitions made."[21]

In the draft cable to Sickles, Fish had left blank the time to comply. Grant suggested fourteen days, but on finding that such a period would leave the administration three days until Congress met on December 1 the Cabinet decided on twelve days. The chance of preserving peace and finding an honorable settlement would be greater if the issue did not fall into the hands of Congress. Each Cabinet member commented on the probability of Spain's meeting the demands. All agreed that the Washington government must settle on a policy that would "satisfy public opinion at home and that of the world."[22] Because there was no certainty the Spanish would be interested in either American or world opinion the Cabinet told Robeson to assemble the navy at Key West. The navy secretary replied, more accurately than before, that "to man all the vessels would require more men than the law allowed," but when Grant and Fish assured him Congress would approve he agreed to take such a step, whether he could or not. In general the Cabinet did not credit the report of a massacre, but if true it would be proof that Spain could not control the island, justification of avenging the wrongs in Cuba.[23] After five years of guerrilla war, burnings, illegal Spanish seizure of ships and property (so the American government believed), lawlessness seemed to be crystallizing.

On November 15, word came from Hall of fifty-three executions. It was reported unofficially that one hundred eleven more men had been shot, with only eighteen passengers and crew escaping death.[24] If Fish had doubt before about Spain's ability to control the island, Hall's telegram swept it away. The secretary cabled Sickles: "If Spain cannot redress the outrage committed in her name the United States will. If Spain should regard this act of self-defense . . . as necessitating her interference, the United States, while regretting it, cannot avoid the results." The restraint he had kept on policy toward Cuba for the past four and one-half years was disappearing. But the dispassionate side of his character reasserted itself: "You will use this instruction cautiously and discreetly, avoiding unnecessarily exciting any proper sensibilities, and avoiding all appearances of menace, but the gravity of the case admits no doubt, and must be fairly and frankly met."[25]

In an effort to learn more he sent for a former consul at Kingston, Thomas Pearne, in charge at the time Captain Fry had taken over the *Virginius*. Pearne assured the secretary that the *Virginius*'s papers were in order when Fry left port. Everything was according to regulation, for Pearne had turned the ship over to Fry at the request, oral and written, of the owner, Quesada.

Fish coldly reminded Pearne that the American, Patterson, was supposed to be the owner.

"So he was," Pearne remarked, "that never occurred to me. Had I thought of that I could not have made the transfer."[26]

The afternoon of November 15, Polo called at Fish's house, in a state of distress. He handed Fish a paper from authorities in Cuba stating that the captured vessel lacked both a crew roll and papers required of merchant vessels. The Madrid government's order to halt the executions could not be carried out because of destruction of the telegraph which the admiral claimed was the work of insurgents. The captain general in Havana had been unable to send instructions to Santiago until November 12. The vessel, Polo added, was a pirate ship. He had the record of the proceedings at Santiago and said the crew had made no secret of their hostile purpose.[27]

Although news of the executions was less than a week old, Fish's reaction had passed through three phases. When he first received word of what had taken place, he regarded it as another incident in a long line of outrages by Spanish against Cubans.[28] Belief that the *Virginius* was an American vessel seized either in British territorial waters or on the high seas caused him to view the capture in terms of an affront to national honor. Then came news of massacre of the crew. He had recoiled from the barbarity of this action and nearly swung to intervention. War, if it came, would rid the island of the plague of the Volunteers who were as much rebels against Spain and humanity as were the separatists. Fish intended action against the Volunteers, not against Spain. Still, if Spain objected—so be it. Finally, based on his conversation with Pearne and reports from Hall and Polo, his doubt about the right of the *Virginius* to fly the American flag reasserted itself. Although he now approached the matter with renewed caution, he still intended to be his nation's advocate, not giving an inch until either the Spanish government proved the truth of the charges or the American government received full restitution.

The American press had observed the development of the crisis, but it was difficult for the State Department to know what press opinion stood for. Newspapers in the United States were in a sort of transition. The year 1872 had marked the end of an era for American journalism. James Gordon Bennett died, his son succeeding as manager of the *New York Herald*. William Cullen Bryant entered into retirement to translate Homer. Horace Greeley of the *Tribune* died. These events symbolized the close of a long period of domination of American politics by party papers. From that point, newspapers were to have a variety of purposes and outlooks, and politics were to be shaped by other means than editorials.[29]

It was a considerable problem for Fish to watch the papers. If they were no longer an extension of parties, they were still influential.[30] And as he well knew, public opinion could influence policy. Already the sensationalism that would mark the yellow press of the 1890s was present in James Gordon Bennett, Jr.'s *Herald* and Charles A. Dana's *New York Sun*.

In the course of the changes in the American newspaper press the only paper in the country to cling to the idea of being a party organ was the *National Republican* of Washington. If the secretary of state expected support from the *Republican,* he was to be disappointed. That journal showed the same split personality that had marked its party's attitude toward Cuba. The editor of the *Republican,* W. J. Murtaugh, had been a spokesman for President Johnson, and Murtaugh perhaps shared the South's pre-Civil War desire for interference in Cuba.[31] The *Republican* began carrying an ad that indicated the threat of war with Spain gave new hope to speculators in Cuban bonds. During the coming session, the notice read, Congress would recognize Cuban independence. "Now is the time to purchase bonds of the Cuban republic. GOOD AS GOLD WHEN CUBA SHALL BE FREE."[32]

If the *Republican* was immoderate, other papers fortunately were slow to anger over seizure of the ship. News of the *Virginius* capture reached New York at the same time as the biennial elections and sentencing of "Boss" William Tweed to prison. The *Times* and *Tribune* at first took a restrained view. Both had supported Fish's policy toward Cuba, and the *Times* editorialized that "A source of considerable trouble to the United States navy and of expense to the government had been removed by the capture of the filibustering steamer *Virginius*." The Spaniards would be able to "bring sufficient proof to procure her condemnation by a prize court."[33] News of Ryan's execution caused the *Times* to decry the barbarous haste of the shootings but the paper maintained a hands-off policy.[34] Additional executions followed by report of a massacre ended moderation. The *New York Evening Post* suggested what Fish had already said to Polo, that Spain might solve its problems with the United States by asking the Americans to undertake a protectorate of the island.[35] The *Times* declared that if Spain had shot Americans illegally "it is a crime for which no explanation or apology can atone. There will be nothing left for the United States government but to declare war. . . "[36] The *Tribune* still viewed Castelar as a friend of the United States but declared that "the Peninsulars are doing the work their victims could never have accomplished. Their muskets are ringing the death knell of Spanish power in America."[37]

All the while James Gordon Bennett, Jr.'s *New York Herald* was trumpeting for expansion, as it had done since the beginning of the Cuban war. It was playing up the most sensational events, and when news lacked color the *Herald* created colorful news. Bennett's commissioning of Henry M. Stanley to "find" the Scottish missionary and explorer David Livingston was an example of his style of dramatic journalism. As a long-time critic of Fish's foreign policy the *Herald* found the secretary's caution open to attack. "It is a duty incumbent upon our government at once to recognize the belligerent rights of the Cubans," it thundered, "and it is a duty which Secretary Fish cannot any longer safely postpone."[38] After the nation thought Spain would massacre the crew, the *Herald* was more nearly correct than it probably knew when it declared, "The crisis has come when, if Mr. Secretary Fish is unequal to meet it, the President will do well to relieve him of the task."[39]

The public mood across the United States seemed to reflect the *Herald*'s war cries. From Boston to New Orleans news of the *Virginius* shook Americans from preoccupation with the business depression which had opened in September, with what later would be called the Panic of 1873. By the time of the *Virginius*'s capture it was becoming apparent that a full-fledged depression was upon the country. As events were to reveal, the depression would last for most of the remaining years of the decade. But men everywhere now bestirred themselves over what they regarded as an insult to their country and joined those few individuals who hitherto had

(65)

worked for intervention out of sympathy for the Cuban cause or to enrich themselves. A series of public meetings occurred to protest the action of Spain and raise the cry for intervention. In New Orleans, General Rafeal Quesada of Cuba, together with former Confederate General James Longstreet, presided over a large crowd. A certain Señor Mendoza rose and asked the people to do something. The time for sorrow was past, he said, the answer now lay in an expedition to avenge the *Virginius*. No one doubted he meant an expedition of American troops. Another speaker was cheered when he declared, "We are on the eve of war." Young ladies in the audience reportedly gave rings, bracelets and other jewelry to the cause.[40] Meetings elsewhere showed a similar enthusiasm. Baltimore witnessed a parade up Main Street with color bearers carrying a Cuban flag draped in mourning, side by side with a U.S. flag. A cheering assemblage in Monument Square passed resolutions demanding belligerent rights for the Cubans. In a public meeting in St. Louis, merchants and citizens urged President Grant to suspend the neutrality laws for sixty to ninety days to "give the people an opportunity to inflict summary vengeance upon the bloodthirsty Spaniards and wrest the island of Cuba from their grasp." In Georgia, crowds in Augusta and Columbus denounced Spain. In Brooklyn a rally urged avenging the insult to the flag, while in Manhattan four thousand Germans met at Germania Hall and advocated a policy of vigor. One Southern editor wrote, "On no occasion for a quarter of a century have the people of all sections of the Union been so united upon a question as upon this of launching the power of our government against the Cuban authorities."[41]

Minister Thornton notified his government: "The appearances are that the affair will drift into hostilities."[42] Around the country reporters were soliciting opinions from prominent men and found that many who previously opposed acquisition of Cuba now favored it. Ex-President Johnson believed Cuba long since should have been annexed. The governor of New Jersey thought the United States should take Cuba. Governor Ingersoll of Connecticut exclaimed that if international law did not furnish a precedent then the country should furnish one for international law.[43] Ex-Governor

(66)

McCook of Colorado Territory expressed the idea in many minds that war would reunite the American nation, still divided by memories of the recent war.[44]

To obtain more information reporters of the *New York Times* interviewed several national figures. Senator Roscoe Conkling, approached at his Fifth Avenue hotel, expressed certainty that the country's honor would be upheld. Many questions remained, he said, concerning the vessel's ownership and right to fly the flag. He blamed the prisoners' deaths on Volunteers who disregarded Spanish orders.[45] Congressmen S. S. Cox of Brooklyn, an interventionist, said there would be no war until Congress met in December. The leader of the New York bar, William M. Evarts, destined to be Fish's successor as secretary of state, did not know until told by reporters that the men had been shot. He asked if that was the news being shouted in the streets during the day. On being told "yes" he was silent for a few minutes, then said he was not familiar enough with the case to express an opinion. Edwards Pierrepont, United States attorney for the southern district of New York, remarked that if the *Virginius* was an American ship there was only one course "and that was to send a fleet to Cuba, bombard its towns," and give the Cubans freedom.[46]

Proponents of intervention planned their most important protest against Spain to take place in New York City. In terms of influential speakers it might move the administration to war. They invited Pierrepont to address the assemblage. An old-time Democrat who had become a Union Democrat and then a supporter of Grant, he now had to choose between demands of the public that he speak and awareness that he must stay in step with the administration. What would be the administration policy? He wrote Fish several letters begging the secretary for advice. He assured Fish he was anxious to do what the administration desired.[47] He told Assistant Secretary of State J. C. Bancroft Davis that several people had approached him for "aid in getting up a meeting about Cuba, and that he had declined." He assured Davis he had impressed upon the Cuban sympathizers that the matter was in the hands of the federal government and "it would not be wise or just in this emergency to take any steps

(67)

without its knowledge and sanction."[48] The same day he wrote Fish of "numerous pressing invitations to speak" and added, "If Washington is as much excited as some citizens of New York appear to be you must have a lively time about Cuba." Perhaps sensing that Fish would not want to intervene he expressed belief that "the excitement here will soon pass off and all honest men will believe that the government knows more about the situation than the people can."[49] Next day he wrote he would keep quiet unless Fish thought his words at the meeting could be useful.[50] Finally he decided the best course was no course and on the same day as the meeting let Fish know: "I shall not attend the meeting."[51]

The pro-Cuban faction would not miss Pierrepont at its meeting, for it seemed they could count on the united support of Wall Street financiers. The nation's money men showed great interest in the *Virginius* affair. Reporters found widespread condemnation of Spain in the street outside the stock exchange. The *Times* reported a large stockholder in a steamship line vowing he would let his ships idle in port and forego all profit for a year if it would avenge the insult. Another gentleman said cynically what many capitalists must have thought — the *Virginius* uproar was the best thing that could have happened, for it would boost business, relieve financial distress, give workers relief in shipyards which already were stepping up work on naval vessels. All businessmen questioned expressed willingness to take temporary losses to get Spain out of Cuba. Their spirit of sacrifice produced a buoyant market and advanced the price of gold.[52]

Reporters found the Navy Department neither as ambiguous as Pierrepont nor as calculating as Wall Street. Rear Admiral David G. Porter was in a talkative mood. "If the flag doesn't protect our ships," he roared, "then the United States should 'haul it in'." Porter made plain he was in no mood to haul in. But the admiral maintained cautiously that the United States should exercise every bit of diplomacy available in the case. "A proper show of politeness is always commendable even as a preliminary to. . . knocking a man down."[53] Spain, he may have calculated, ranked fifth among the world's navies at that time, while the United States was not even tenth.

About this time the *New York Times* noted that the size of the American navy made it difficult to reinforce squadrons. The navy had ships it "would not care to put to sea."[54] Too many were wooden-hulled. As *The Nation* observed, "The huge wooden screws which we send cruising around the world. . . and which are paraded in newspapers as terrible engines of war, are almost useless for military purposes. They belong to a class of ships which other governments have sold or are selling for firewood."[55] The two largest vessels of the navy each carried about forty guns. The *Juniata*, alerted for Cuban duty, was just back from an Arctic voyage and undergoing repairs. The *Kansas,* in Cuban waters, was nothing but a rowboat of five or six guns. By drawing ships from the Mediterranean squadron the United States could muster about twenty-five vessels for Atlantic duty.

Critics notwithstanding, Rear Admiral Rowan of the Brooklyn Navy Yard said he would work on ships night and day to get them ready. "We have men of experience and we have the dash in the United States." If it came to a fight the United States could "whip" Spain.[56]

General Sherman did not bother arguing the case for the United States army. Talk about going to war over the *Virginius* was absurd, he said, for the army, down from its huge Civil War strength to perhaps 35,000 men, was "entirely inadequate."[57]

President Grant began to receive offers from ex-officers around the country to raise regiments. In New York an independent group, the Emmet Legion, offered the services of eight hundred men at twenty-four hours' notice. From Chicago an ex-lieutenant declared, "One thousand old soldiers are ready at your service in defense of our flag." Nor would it be only ex-members of the Union army, for a colonel in New Orleans wired Grant he would be "ready when called on to furnish seven hundred confederates and five hundred union men for war with Spain." From Savannah came a telegram signed by a committee that a meeting had denounced Spain and "five thousand colored citizens are ready to enlist for Cuba to teach the Spanish authorities respect for the American flag."[58]

There was evidence of a certain fervor. On November 14

the *London Times* correspondent reported that "rarely has a more universal feeling of indignation and surprise animated the American people than that which was caused by the telegram from Cuba. . . announcing additional executions." The deaths in Cuba had produced a "pitch of righteous anger" not felt since the guns had fired on Sumter twelve years before.[59] Thornton again reported to London that the *Virginius* affair could lead to war. "The two countries," he wrote Granville, "have long been on the eve of a rupture, and the affair of the *Virginius* is but the additional hair which seems likely to break the camel's back."[60]

Fish knew that if he could keep Grant's support he could maintain peace, but Grant frequently could be swayed when Fish was not around. Members of Grant's family were in league with the secretary of state's enemies. On a train trip from Washington to New York, Bancroft Davis encountered Grant's brother-in-law, General Frederick Dent, who had begun the ride "so drunk he couldn't speak plainly." Dent had espied Davis and come up demanding in a loud voice, "What are you going to do with the *Virginius*?" Davis sought to turn the conversation, but Dent kept returning to it. "You may pretend not to know. . . that's all right for you. . . but I know all about it." Dent claimed he had been present at the last Cabinet meeting and heard what was said. "I hope we shan't stand this," he roared, his pronunciation blurred. "I want to be sent down there with my battery. I shall like nothing better than to pitch into Morro Castle." Fortunately his speech, Davis believed, was unintelligible to most bystanders. Dent left the train at Newark, staggering through the station to the Manhattan ferry.[61]

This was the talk, personal and national, unofficial and otherwise, when at Steinway Hall in New York on the night of November 17, with rain falling, the doors opened at 7:30 and in a few minutes all seats were taken. Those who could not get in stood in the drenching rain and cheered public figures as they arrived. A meeting was organized at Tammany Hall to accomodate the overflow.[62] Inside the hall flickering gaslights on walls and ceilings illuminated a scene of shouting and stomping for the men seated on the speakers' platform. The wet crowd was in a hot mood. Chairman and first

(70)

speaker of the meeting was the tall, gaunt William Evarts. It was the moment for a fighting speech, the crowd was ready, but the Steinway meeting then turned out to be a fairly mild affair. It became evident that Evarts would not inflame. He limited his words to an attack on officials in Cuba and on the Peninsulars. "If it is true. . . that the power of Spain no longer controls the actions of the Cubans, if it is true that these have all the responsibility of a regular warfare, we shall see to it that they do not also have all the immunities of regulated authority."[63] The American government felt the same way they did, and Spain would be held to account. He said nothing more; in Evarts's hands the meeting quieted. The meeting next heard and adopted a resolution incorporating Thomas Jefferson's words of 1793 when the nation's first secretary of state had written the Spanish representative in Philadelphia with regard to Creek Indians killing American citizens in Spanish Florida: "If Spain chooses to consider our defense against savage butchery as a cause of war to her, we must meet her also in war, with regret but without fear."[64] Then came telegrams from Vice President Henry Wilson, the Reverend Henry Ward Beecher, and other prominent men.[65] Finally the meeting which had threatened far more than it delivered, adjourned.

Leadership for peace outside the administration came from several dissenting spirits of the day, chief among them Charles Sumner, senior senator from Massachusetts and former head of the Foreign Relations Committee. The tall, arrogant Sumner had been an abolitionist and after the Civil War had fought President Johnson and then threw away a friendship with Grant over issues of foreign policy. As vindictive as Sumner, Grant had secured his removal from the chairmanship of the Foreign Relations Committee. Sumner became increasingly critical of the President and broke also with Fish. As a liberal Republican he had championed the Spanish republican experiment. While he sympathized with the Cuban rebels he nevertheless realized the weakness of that movement, and refused to support the forces for intervention and annexation.[66] To learn what he thought of the *Virginius* affair a *New York Tribune* reporter journeyed up to his house in Boston. Sumner was out. After searching

(71)

through the neighborhood the reporter found him in a public library. Yes, Sumner said, he knew of the Steinway Hall meeting, but was unable to attend, although he had sent a telegram. Always suspecting treachery he added, "I suppose I shall be attacked for what I have written unless they suppress the letter." When the reporter questioned him as to what he thought of the seizure of the *Virginius*, Sumner replied that the facts showed the vessel flew the American flag. Even if the flag was flying it made no difference in the vessel's mission. The flag could not change the ship's illegal nature. "I might call myself Castelar, or Emperor of Germany, but I am still Charles Sumner." Although he sympathized with the Cubans he thought it would be foolish to make the *Virginius* affair a plea for recognition of Cuban independence. The first business of the United States should be to save the Spanish republic. Enemies of republicanism around the world would like nothing better than to see two of the world's republics destroy each other. Britain especially, Sumner believed, disliked the Spanish republic and would like to have it crushed by the United States.[67]

Cooler heads had begun considering alternatives. E. L. Godkin's *Nation,* a periodical which could be counted on to oppose jingoism, admitted that if the Spanish government shot men illegally there must be an apology and punishment. But there could be no doubt that the vessel carried Cubans bound for the guerrillas, and the *Nation* insisted the *Virginius* "was not a bona-fide American vessel."[68] Among Southern newspapers the feeling expressed by the *Savannah News* and the *Richmond Whig* predominated. The *News* feared that desire for war was "becoming more general, pervading all classes of all sections." War seemed likely, but it would be a war in which "Spain has all to lose, and the United States nothing to gain." The *Whig* expressed a conviction that the nation was lucky to have Fish heading foreign affairs and urged patience.[69] The *Atlanta Constitution* editorialized that the Southern press was speaking as one against the outrage but believed it was time to be calm, for war would injure the Southerners' recovery from their own war. A letter to the editor of the *New Orleans Picayune* showed that at least some individuals thought there was little purpose in a Cuban war. According to this writer the South was more interested in justice at home than in Spanish colonies.[70]

From New York the expansionist *Herald* did everything possible to rally the war party, even declaring that most of the country's religious press, Catholic and Protestant, was in a mood for fighting. But the *Christian Union*, one of the more important Protestant periodicals, appealed to the nation which, "in the great Arbitration, set the example and gave the hope of a better day" to meet the new crisis "with a union of firmness and self-control worthy of that good record."[71]

Admittedly there were forces arrayed in favor of peace. Many men believed that a war with Spain would be the greatest evil that could befall a nation afflicted with the problems of reconstruction. Idealists regarded the beleaguered republic of Castelar as a nation in distress, deserving of aid and not enmity. From his office in the Department of State, Hamilton Fish would recover his aplomb and seek to guide affairs along the pacific ways. But there was sentiment for war, even within the American diplomatic establishment. Fish would have to deal, among other problems, with the flamboyant, bellicose Sickles who from the vantage point of Madrid might attempt to shove American foreign policy in a war-like direction.

CHAPTER SIX

Madrid

THERE were few things Daniel Sickles enjoyed more than a good military ceremony. Once in Spain he took every opportunity to show that he had been in a war. On the day of the capture of the *Virginius* he was playing his military role in a ceremony in which Spain's minister of war, General Sanchez Brequa, presented to the President of the United States (Sickles acting as intermediary) a fine Toledo blade as a mark of good will from the Spanish government. Sickles described the sword to Fish as:

> A regulation Cavalry model with elaborately chased scroll-work in raised steel on a ground of dead gold. On one side is a scroll enveloping an olive-branch with the inscription, "Let us have Peace." On the other, a similar scroll, having within its folds a spray of laurel, bears the names of the more prominent battles in which General Grant took part.[1]

Still Sickles's position in Madrid was not entirely satisfactory, for even prior to arrival in Spain his reputation had preceded him in the form of a pamphlet in Spanish relating unsavory episodes in his career.[2] So, while the government gave Sickles the honors due his position, the better families carefully withheld social recognition.

There were other problems, such as Spanish diplomatic procedures, which frustrated him as it did everyone in Madrid. One difficulty of negotiating with the Spanish government was summed up in a remark attributed to Britain's Lord Clarendon: "Spanish dynasties go and come, Spanish queens go and come, and Spanish Ministries go and come, but there is one thing in Spain that is always the same—they never answer letters." Sickles believed that President Castelar wanted to abolish slavery and adopt a more liberal policy toward Cuba, but that he was dependent on other leaders and bound to respect their hostility toward Cuban independence.[3] He wrote Fish that the government had shown no evidence it could survive. The shuffling of Cabinets was responsible for his failure to achieve more concessions on the Cuban question. "With each successive Cabinet I am obliged to begin anew all pending negotiations. Every colonial minister must first study and mature his colonial policy, and it generally happens that he goes out of office before he determines what to do."[4]

When word of the *Tornado*'s exploit arrived in the capital on November 6, Sickles went to meet with Minister of State José de Carvajal to suggest "an opportunity to inaugurate a more generous and humane policy in Cuba."[5] Carvajal was absent, so the American minister contented himself with giving this message to a deputy and writing a private note. That evening he went to the Executive Palace to interview President Castelar. He had no instructions and the United States had no desire to protect the enemies of Spain, but if the *Virginius* was an American ship then his government would demand return both of the ship and all individuals on board. He reminded Castelar of previous summary executions in Cuba and recommended an order forbidding such proceedings. The President received the advice "with his usual kindness" and said that when the cable from Cuba had arrived that morning he had sent such a message.[6]

Fish on November 8 sent news of the execution of Ryan and companions, and again Sickles hurried to the Ministry of State where he told Carvajal of Fish's cable and expressed regret that the incident showed the expediency of the steps he had recommended. Carvajal had no information. Sickles pressed the case. There would have been no question if the *Virginius* had been in Spanish waters and a fair trial given the men under Article VII of Pinckney's Treaty of 1795, but the *Tornado* had exceeded its jurisdiction in capturing a ship flying a foreign flag on the open seas. Spanish ships-of-war had no more right to lay hands on an American vessel at sea than the United States to enter Cadiz and arrest a fugitive from American justice. Carvajal assured Sickles that the administration would take up the question of the *Virginius* and decide it on principles of public law uninfluenced by passion.[7]

Sickles returned to the legation, but while writing to Fish found his work interrupted by an aide announcing the arrival of Carvajal. The Spaniard hurried into the room saying, "I have bad news; four of the party on board the *Virginius* have been shot." The Madrid government, he said, expressed "utmost concern and regret" but was certain, if the information was correct, that it happened before receipt of orders sent to the captain general by Castelar. The whole matter, Carvajal assured the American, would receive attention from the Council of Ministers.[8]

Carvajal later informed Sickles he had not yet obtained the report requested from the captain general. Sickles decided to take his case to the president of the republic. On the night of November 10, 1873, the carriage of the minister clattered up to the executive mansion, and the president welcomed Sickles exclaiming, "How deeply I deplore the execution of the four prisoners at Santiago de Cuba! What a misfortune that my order was not received in time to prevent such an act! It was against the law, and the only excuse offered is that a sentence of death had already been pronounced against these men." An aide interrupted, but Castelar did not use the opportunity to change the subject. "Such scandals must cease," he proclaimed. Spain's greatest orator was by now warmed for one of his famous monologues. It was not Burriel who killed the men, he continued, but slavery. That morning, he claimed, he had told a conservative delegation that Cuban slavery must end, for "it brutalized all it touches." Sickles replied that such an offense against civilization must have punishment. He pressed for an end to slavery: abolition would remove the cause of other barbarities. Castelar assured Sickles that the government would investigate as soon as the captain general's answers could be considered by the Council of Ministers.[9]

For the next several days Sickles waited, and on the evening of November 12 received a visit from Carvajal accompanied by the under secretary of state. Information from Cuba, the foreign minister recounted, indicated the *Tornado* had sighted the *Virginius* attempting to land cargo and passengers; a pursuit had followed, resulting in capture about twenty-three miles from Jamaica. Carvajal at first alleged the

Virginius carried no papers but qualified this by stating that its documents were not authorized by any consul and were irregular. Downplaying the seriousness of the case, he expressed confidence that it would be much less difficult to adjust than first believed. The Spanish administration was gratified to learn that Sickles's reports had influenced Secretary Fish. With satisfaction they had read Polo's reports of conversations with Fish. Polo's dispatches spoke of excitement now "perceptibly diminished" in view of more information. The minister ended by inviting Sickles to the palace the next afternoon for a conference.[10] Sickles assured Carvajal that whatever the popular outcry in the United States provoked by capture of the *Virginius,* it would not influence President Grant in a matter affecting relations with a friendly power.[11]

Whatever hope the two men might have had for settling the dispute ended next afternoon when Sickles called at four o'clock, as Carvajal received him with the remark that late news from Cuba would deprive the conference of success. The captain general had reported the shooting of forty-nine additional prisoners on November 7 and 8.[12] Castelar's orders had arrived too late. Unfortunately, he explained, laws passed in September forbidding the death penalty for civilians without executive approval were inoperative in Cuba. He assured the American that the slaughter had stopped, for Captain General Jovellar was holding himself responsible for enforcement of Castelar's instruction.[13]

The two men began fencing over the question of liability for the deaths. Sickles demanded to know if Spanish statutes had no force in Cuba. Carvajal replied that he had only expressed an opinion that the republic's laws were inapplicable. Sickles repeated his belief that if execution of American citizens in Santiago had occurred "without respecting the rights guaranteed to the accused in all trials for offenses charged against them," after the United States again and again had insisted on these obligations, responsibility was on the Spanish government.[14] With Sickles's charges becoming more barbed Carvajal must have feared trouble, for he said he could not "in the present state of the question. . .proceed with the discussion."[15]

Sickles stubbornly continued the attack. He called attention to a Havana bulletin of November 5 which announced that trials of the *Virginius*'s crew were in progress. From this he assumed that four days had elapsed between capture of the ship and its arrival in port. "An interval of four days," he told Carvajal, "was inconsistent with the statement of the captain general that it was taken only a few miles from Jamaica." The speed of the prisoners' execution indicated they had not received a trial. The Spaniard replied that in cases of the trial and sentencing of prisoners in absentia it was only necessary to identify them. Sickles again objected. The minister of state's predecessor in office had assured the United States government that according to Spanish law such sentences could not be carried out when parties demanded a hearing. At any rate the United States had declared it would not recognize the trial and sentencing of an American citizen without presence of the accused.[16] To this, Carvajal said nothing.

At three o'clock next day, the fourteenth, Sickles presented the Spanish minister of state with a note of protest against "the said act of the authorities in Cuba as barbarous and brutal, and an outrage upon this epoch of civilization. The United States will demand the most ample reparation of any wrong which may have been thereby committed upon any of its citizens or upon its flag."[17] The note carried out Fish's instructions of November 12.

On the fifteenth, Fish's cable arrived outlining four demands that amounted to an ultimatum. The secretary demanded the *Virginius*'s return, release of its crew, a salute to the flag, and punishment of officials "concerned in the capture of the vessel and the execution of the passengers and crew." If the Spanish refused, and declined reparation by November 26, Sickles was to close the legation and leave.[18]

Immediately afterward another cable reached Sickles. It contained the erroneous report that Cuban authorities had shot fifty-seven crew members and only eighteen had escaped the firing squad. Fish wrote that if Spain could not maintain order in Cuba, the United States would, and "if Spain should regard this act of self-defense. . .as necessitat-

(79)

ing her interference, the United States, while regretting it cannot avoid the result." The secretary ordered Sickles to "use this instruction cautiously and discreetly. . .avoiding all appearance of menace; but the gravity of the case admits no doubt, and must be fairly and frankly met."[19]

Like a battle, diplomacy can be confusing to participants, who seldom can see the whole picture, and Sickles by November 15 was acting on three false premises: he had mistaken the time between capture and arrival of the prisoners in Santiago; he believed only a few hours had elapsed between arrival and execution; and he as well as the government in Washington believed Cuban officials had shot all but eighteen of the passengers and crew. The actions of Washington must have encouraged him. Nearly twenty years had passed since the Ostend Manifesto, nearly five since the beginning of the Cuban war that was violating American rights. Finally it seemed as if the United States, prodded by the *Virginius* affair, would put energy to the task of acquiring Cuba.

But the Spanish government was responding to the crisis in its own way and, like the American, reacting only to matters within its own line of vision. To Carvajal the seizure and executions had seemed one more irritation arising out of troubled Cuba, but as he began to receive protests his mood changed. The argument Sickles made seemed an accusation of guilt. It was the same interference that America had been undertaking for years in what Carvajal and most Spaniards considered their domestic affairs. Carvajal had only to look about him to realize that defiance would be popular. The Spanish press was divided between denunciation of the United States, including its representative at Madrid, and praise of the authorities in Cuba.[20] The same day he received Sickles's protest he sat down to reply that the Spanish republic would not recognize Sickles's competency to make the protest, because the government lacked facts in the case. Indeed the minister of state treated the protest as though Sickles were acting on his own and not as a representative of the United States.[21] Sickles fired off a rejoinder saying that he was not surprised that the Spanish government while declaring the United States lacked sufficient information on the in-

(80)

cident, "at the same moment denounces the unfortunate victims ... and applauds the chief actors in the bloody tragedy."[22]

At this point the British government entered the dispute. While Sickles and his Spanish counterpart engaged in a verbal contest that could lead to war, a cable arrived from London informing the British Minister, Sir Austin Henry Layard, that sixteen subjects were among the victims in Santiago.[23] When news had first reached London it had created less sensation than in America; there was not the same proximity as between the United States and Cuba, and it was thought no British subjects were aboard the ship.[24] Consul John Crawford's report to London dispelled that illusion and Prime Minister William Gladstone's Cabinet agreed to cable Madrid, Havana, and Santiago that "We shall hold the Spanish government, and all persons concerned, strictly liable for any further executions under the circumstances which have been stated."[25] Granville left the problem of negotiating with Spain in the hands of Layard.

Sir Austin had arrived in Madrid in 1869 after a career which saw him rise from a modest place in Victorian society to fame and a knighthood. Largely self-taught, he had excavated the ancient Assyrian cities of Nineveh and Nimrud. During the 1860s he had served as a Liberal member of Parliament. He spoke Spanish as well as Sickles, and was even more blunt, for he shared his contemporaries' outlook that God was an Englishman. Yet as his biographer has related, he made "a great success of his mission, partly because he disliked the Spaniards so much that he did not get involved in their politics."[26] After passing through the tumult of one revolution after another he had declared Spaniards "about as fit for universal suffrage and constitutional government as Fiji Islanders."[27] The Carlist wars and the insurrection at Cartagena had caused problems between Spain and Britain similar to those the Cuban war was creating with the United States. London papers were full of complaints from Englishmen under fire in Spain, such as the merchant at Cartagena whose house had been hit by cannon fire and who complained of "the misfortune to be a British subject."[28]

When Layard went for an audience with President Castelar

he found the Chief Executive looking worn and troubled from problems of health and government. Layard related the reason for his visit and Castelar became "greatly agitated," for it was the first he had heard of British deaths and he had hoped for Britain's sympathy in his troubles. The president argued that the *Virginius* was a pirate vessel that had no right to the flag of the United States.[29] Layard replied that the crew of the *Virginius* were not pirates and could only be charged with running a blockade.[30] Castelar seemed momentarily persuaded that the men were not pirates and in Layard's presence wrote a cable to Captain General Jovellar ordering him to protect British subjects. The president appealed to Jovellar's patriotism to save Spain from a quarrel with its old ally. Castelar swore he was determined to put an end to the efforts of the Volunteers to destroy the authority of the Madrid government.[31]

The President of Spain thus had the double shock of finding he could not depend on British aid, and learning that Sickles had delivered a virtual ultimatum. Like many Spaniards he had believed that the British government would prefer to keep Americans out of the Caribbean, and undaunted he set out to enlist Britain's aid the same evening that Layard had visited him with news that Britain was now a party to the dispute. He had admitted his alarm to the bewhiskered Layard, and asked for sympathy. A rupture with the United States was "inevitable," he declared.[32] Spanish public opinion would force him to fight the Yankees. There was one hope: if Her Majesty's government would join its demand for reparations with that of the United States. Then, he reasoned, it would be less humiliating to Spain to yield to two great powers, "one of which could not be suspected of any design upon Cuba." If Britain was unwilling to take this course then he requested that it act as arbiter of the dispute.[33] Skeptical, Layard cabled the Foreign Office of the Spanish request and next morning the British Cabinet agreed to discuss the matter.[34]

Layard had informed Granville that the chances for peace between the United States and Spain seemed bleak. The next day, November 17, he saw his American counterpart, whose intentions he had learned to distrust, and found Sickles in a talkative mood. Balancing himself on his crutch (he seldom wore his artificial leg) the American minister spoke about the Spanish attitude. He was certain the United States would have to take action, because Spain would not. Layard thought Sickles in a dangerous mood and attempted to calm him.[35]

On the seventeenth Castelar returned to Layard for the British government's answer to his request, either to join its claims with those of the United States or serve as arbiter, even though Layard from the outset of Spain's troubles with the Americans had impressed the Spanish president that Britain would give no aid to Spain in the event of war with America. But Granville had dashed whatever hope he had by telegraphing to Layard the Cabinet's refusal. There was no reason to think America would want joint action; nor could Britain oblige Spain by acting as an arbiter, for, said Granville, it was his government's belief that satisfaction was due the United States, and Britain was party to the claim which would have to be arbitrated.[36] Layard did not mention that the British Cabinet was concerned over the effects of a Spanish-American war on commerce and fearful British shipping would suffer from Spanish privateers.[37] After hearing this news Castelar asked Layard for advice, which the Englishman was willing to give: "Release the *Virginius* at once," and punish those persons responsible for the executions. Playing on the Spaniard's pride Layard asked if the president had courage to defy press attacks and hostility from the Volunteers in Cuba. If he did then he ought to instruct the captain general to "bring the assassins to justice." Castelar replied he was ready to follow the recommendations, though there was still a question as to the *Virginius*'s right to fly the United States flag.[38] After the president left, Layard wrote Granville sarcastically that Castelar wished to do the right thing "but as usual he cannot decide upon taking the bold and only right course."[39]

Conditions forced Castelar to take a bold course if he wished to prevent war. The Madrid press attacked the United States, Sickles, and Britain with equal ferocity, and seemed to Layard to be "doing its utmost to drive the country into a war with the United States & England too."[40] The Britisher went to Castelar and asked him to halt this newspaper campaign, and the president called together the leading journalists of Madrid, appealed to their patriotism, and in case this was insufficient initiated legal proceedings against papers that attacked Sickles. This was likely to be effective. As Layard commented, "Every one knows what legal proceedings in Spain mean."[41] The newspapers lifted their barrage against Britain but sought to show a difference between the two nations' approach to the *Virginius* question. It seemed that on government orders the press was contrasting the behavior of Britain with that of the United States.[42] *Discussion* on November 18 informed its readers that Britain would not act in hostile fashion toward a friendly nation and *Igualidad* the same day proclaimed that Spain had nothing to fear from a nation which in the past had hung pirates from the yardarms of its ships.

Circumstances favoring settlement through the efforts of Castelar now seemed at an end, for on the eighteenth the president returned to the British legation to tell Layard that the previous night the Council of State had decided the *Virginius* could not be given up until full inquiry proved the capture illegal. He assured Layard that after investigation Spain would offer satisfaction to the United States. He already had telegraphed Admiral Polo in Washington to ask President Grant to suspend action on the case for such time as was "absolutely necessary" to make the investigation.[43]

By the eighteenth the Spanish government had received denials from Cuba that additional shootings had taken place or a massacre had occurred or was intended. Carvajal wrote another blistering note. "One fact alone is. . .admitted by all the world. The *Virginius,* which has already a lamentable reputation in the Cuban struggles, had been equipped in order to aid the insurrection, in the territory of a friendly nation."[44] Sickles was furious and told Layard he did not know what would satisfy the United States after the manner in which he had been treated. He thought it likely he would be recalled by Washington and have to leave Madrid next day.[45]

All the while Carvajal was handing out copies of his notes to Sickles to six friendly editors who praised him for defending Spain's honor against the Yankee adventurer.[46] He became the darling of Spaniards who wanted to confront the

United States. As ill-fitted for his post as was Sickles, particularly during a crisis, the foreign minister was composing some of the drafts of his dispatches to Cuba in the Café Fornos where to the applause of admirers he read the more stirring passages aloud.[47] The Spaniard was treating Sickles's protests as if they were merely Sickles's own views and not those of the American government.[48]

By Wednesday, November 19, Sickles was nearly beside himself because of Spanish insults. The same rage that once drove him to rush through Lafayette Square to kill a man was driving him to search for a way to strike at the Spanish republic. He had always been involved in plots with agents of the Cuban revolution in Madrid, and now was less discreet.[49] The *Diario Español* reported a "bird of ill omen" (Sickles) seen prowling around the Barrio de Pozes, a slum neighborhood where Cuban agents resided. On the night of the eighteenth a mob assembled to march on the American legation. Troops intervened and the mob dispersed.[50] Thus two weeks after Ryan and his companions fell in the first executions at Santiago, it seemed that only war could resolve the troubles between the two republics.

CHAPTER SEVEN

The Thanksgiving Protocol

THE United States government enjoyed large international support and sympathy for its difficulties with Spain over the *Virginius*. The British public and Foreign Office backed the Americans. Even newspapers which usually could be counted on to cry "foul" when Brother Jonathan showed an aggressive spirit were subdued in comment on Spanish-American relations.[1] From the legation in Berlin the historian-minister George Bancroft wrote that the administration's policy "is universally approved of both as to its substance and its form." He enclosed favorable essays by a German professor of international law. "Our best friends here," he said, "trust that we may escape the misfortune of annexing Cuba," for they believed what was also a widespread thought in the United States, that the island with its large black and mulatto population would prove "absolutely unmanageable."[2] Spain's northern neighbor France agreed. Paris journals referred to the United States's "Spanish difficulty." Monarchical journals used the crisis as an opportunity to declare that if Don Carlos were on the throne such things would not happen, while the republican press thought it the duty of the United States not to destroy a sister republic. Annexation found support in journals controlled by followers of the deposed Napoleon III. According to the Bonapartists, America had every right to stop such massacres and every thinking man would approve annexation. The Spaniards were distinctly in disfavor in Paris, Berlin, and London. The Paris correspondent of the *New York Times* reported in mid-November that "Señor Castelar has just written to his friends here to take the sentimental line, and to cry out immediately and as loud as possible. He does not put it in that way, but it amounts to the same thing."[3]

If European opinion was favorable, it did not make the secretary of state's task easier. When Thornton called on Fish to deliver Granville's request that America give Spain more time, the secretary honestly could reply that this had already been done "to a certain extent." He confessed his fear that Sickles had put the demands "in rather hard language" and had proposed to leave Madrid on the nineteenth even though not instructed. The greatest favor Britain could do, Fish said, would be to urge Castelar to come to a settlement before Congress met in December.[4] Fish showed no more than cautious optimism when later questioned by the Mexican minister. He hoped to avoid a rupture but "I cannot speak with confidence."[5]

There had been some confusion over what had happened. Washington had received Hall's report that nearly the entire crew had been shot. An ultimatum had followed to Madrid. Then a report from Hall of no general massacre; stories of eighty members of the *Virginius* being shot were erroneous.[6]

Hope had appeared when Polo brought news of a softening. A telegram had arrived, Polo explained, in which his government promised to abide by law, comply with treaties, and punish guilty parties regardless of rank.

Compared with reports from Sickles the promises offered by Polo seemed the height of diplomacy. Sickles was reporting Carvajal's decision that no reparation would be offered until Spain was satisfied an offense had taken place.[7] At the Cabinet meeting of November 18, Fish relayed Spain's offer and request for an extension of time before Sickles closed the legation. The United States must be sure it was in the right; there were too many questions. Rumor had it that the ship belonged to Cubans rather than Americans, and he mentioned his interview with the former consul at Kingston, Pearne. If Quesada was the owner then Pearne had erred in giving the vessel American papers. He read a letter from Captain Edwin L. Brady who had been approached by the Cubans some years earlier to sail the *Virginius*. Grant said there would be time enough before the twenty-sixth to decide whether to extend the deadline. Fish cabled Sickles, recounted the Polo interview, and ordered the minister to lower his voice.[8]

By this time the British government had become involved. The Spanish offer, it turned out, had originated not only with

Castelar but with Layard, anxious as he watched Sickles. Reminding the Spanish president that he could expect no help from Britain, Layard increased the pressure on Castelar to agree to the American demands.[9] There was nothing to gain and much to lose by allowing Carvajal and Sickles to carry on their argument. The time had come for the president to negotiate with Fish through Admiral Polo, bypassing Sickles and Carvajal.[10] Castelar hesitated. For days he had lived with fear that Sickles would leave Madrid, and believed the American would carry out the threat to close the legation if he knew he was no longer negotiating. Layard did not think Sickles would leave and persuaded Castelar that the minister could be controlled.[11] By the eighteenth a nervous Spanish executive was ready to begin offering compromises to Washington. By the nineteenth all communication between Sickles and the Spanish government had ceased.[12]

A problem facing Castelar was the possibility that the Conservative Party under Marshal Francisco Serrano would attempt to make political capital out of any backing down by the Liberals, but Layard helped Castelar find a solution. During the coup which overthrew the monarchy of King Amadeo I in February, 1873, Layard at Castelar's request had helped Serrano escape from the Madrid mob.[13] On November 19 the general came to the British legation to ask about the *Virginius*. At first Serrano, like Castelar, Polo, and most Spaniards, had considered the *Virginius* a pirate ship. After Layard presented the facts of the case he seemed to change his mind and said the executions had been a violation of international law. Serrano realized as well as Castelar that a war with the United States would end in disaster and pledged to stop any conservative attack on Castelar's policies. Layard attached importance to Serrano's help and wrote Granville that although things had been bleak there was more hope.[14]

News of a change in attitude by Spain must have been surprising to Sickles. If the matter were settled by diplomacy, then the island of Cuba, which Sickles believed rightfully belonged to the United States, would remain Spanish. Success would belong to Fish; for Sickles there would be no triumphant return to the United States to the cheers of his countrymen, no presidency to win. But it was not the time to lose

(89)

one's head with so much at risk, and on the day he received word that the Spanish government might be bypassing him he sent two telegrams. The first told of a message from Carvajal. "Neither this nor either of the three communications in writing so far received contains any expression of regret or disapproval of the capture or the slaughter at Santiago. The press approves the whole business, and denies that any censure or regret had been expressed by this government. The ministerial journals acquiesce."[15] In the second telegram he turned to the matter at hand. The "tone, temper, and substance" of communication from Carvajal were "very different from the apparent purport of the telegram sent to the Spanish minister in Washington and communicated to you." Carvajal's notes were, he believed, "the real position of this government." If Spain's duplicity were rewarded, the government would be more arrogant. A peaceful solution in Washington would "corroborate the intimation made here" that his actions in the *Virginius* affair did not conform to instructions and were not approved by Washington. It would be best if he withdrew from Madrid, which action would "convince Spain we are in earnest, and she will yield to our terms and peace may be honorably preserved." The Spanish government was presenting different attitudes in Madrid and Washington, to gain time. He ended by describing his plan to place American interests in the hands of the Italian chargé when he left the country.[16]

Friday, November 21, in Washington, opened on a note of optimism. Thornton called on Fish to report a dispatch from London: Granville had telegraphed Layard to urge Castelar to comply; Layard had sent news he was sure Spain wanted to accede and hoped time could be granted.[17]

The same day Fish took his carriage to the White House for a Cabinet meeting, where discussion centered on the Spanish proposal of turning the *Virginius* affair over to arbitration. Fish's diary gives only the outline of what must have been a long discussion. It was decided that arbitration as proposed could not be agreed upon. The matter was a question of national honor, too serious to admit a third-party decision. The nation which in the Geneva accord with Britain had set a standard for arbitration in the nineteenth century showed how seriously it regarded the Cuban situation by refusing to follow its own precedent. Still, Fish was told to tell Polo to hold the door open for negotiation. The Cabinet decided to deny Sickles's request for a ship to take him and family to Valencia.[18]

The same afternoon a message went out from the State Department directing Sickles in no uncertain language to take orders from Washington. If a difference existed between proposals made by Spain at Madrid and those offered in Washington, President Grant felt it proper to consider "the representations made at Washington" which most nearly complied with United States demands. The president "depends upon you to cooperate with our efforts to induce Spain to make such concessions as may avert a rupture between the two republics, without questioning the sincerity of the Madrid Cabinet."[19] When he received this instruction Sickles must have cursed the administration in general and the secretary of state in particular. Spanish deceit was winning over his best efforts: the Grant administraton preferred to believe the Spanish rather than his warnings.

There can be no doubt that Sickles hoped for war. His dealings with Carvajal gave the impression that the foreign minister spoke for his government. But the foreign minister could not believe that Sickles spoke for Washington. In their abrasive exchanges Sickles found justification for believing Spain more willing to give battle than reparations.[20] In a letter to Benjamin Moran, secretary of the legation in London, he wrote that "I hope the nuisance of Spanish dominion in America will be now and forever ended. I suppose I shall have taken my leave before you receive this. How the old time comes back to me while I write this to you."[21]

Then at last the Spanish backed down. At 2:00 a.m. on November 26 (November 25, Washington time) a message came to Sickles from Castelar saying a note would be sent that day recognizing the principles on which the United States based its demands. If the *Virginius* proved an American ship, the Spanish president promised reparation by Christmas.

There followed a minor contretemps. The general had replied that delay would be unacceptable, but dutifully added

(91)

that on receipt of a note accepting the American demands he would send it to the department and defer leaving Madrid. Not that he thought the note would be anything but another example of the "deceitful don." Several hours later, no message from Carvajal having been received, he cabled Fish that the delay was "to gain time to strengthen the Spanish fleet in the Gulf of Mexico and send troops to Cuba, and that at last some pretext will be found to evade the reparation. The fall of Cartagena, which is daily looked for, is expected to liberate the home squadron and the besieging army."[22] That afternoon, with only silence from the Spanish ministry, Sickles sent Alvey Adee to get the passports. Adee waited to be ushered into Carvajal's office. To bear a note from the Tycoon to Carvajal asking for passports was unpleasant work. What he thought of his boss's handling of the diplomacy he did not record. He placed the note in Carvajal's hands. The Spaniard showed surprise. He had sent the American minister a note that day, he told Adee; had Sickles received his note before asking for the passports? Nothing, Adee replied, had been received up to the time he, Adee, had left the legation.[23] Carvajal's timing had been close. While Sickles awaited Adee's return with the passports, a courier had handed the American minister a note containing the substance of Castelar's early morning message. Spain bound itself to salute the American flag and return the ship and crew if it could not prove the ship flew the American flag illegally. If authorities at Santiago had infringed foreign rights, they would be brought before "competent tribunals." Unwilling to give up the idea of arbitration, the Madrid government held out the promise of settlements of other questions between the two governments which, if not solvable by negotiation, would be submitted to a mutually satisfactory third party.

After attending church Secretary and Mrs. Fish spent the rest of Thanksgiving Day, November 27, at home. President Grant also attended church, and on return to the Executive Mansion found some of his old military friends, Generals Sheridan, Babcock, and others, present to converse on his favorite subject, the late war. This day the talk was not of past wars but of future ones. A member of Elihu Washburne's Paris legation, John Del Montaigne, was present. Armed with an introduction from Washburne, Montaigne found Grant charming. He wrote Washburne that there was "a real council of war," not about war, of course, "but the men were there who would wipe out the whole of Spain and Cuba with their butcherers without trouble." Grant had shown Montaigne several letters he had received concerning the *Virginius,* from men anxious to procure commissions in event of war. Some were from former rebels. The "threat of war," Montaigne concluded, "seems to have awakened a regard for the old flag."[24]

While Grant and friends held council, Fish was receiving the emissary of peace, for Polo called at the Fish residence shortly after noon and heard the latest Spanish proposals received from Sickles. They were impossible, said Fish. The status of the *Virginius* could not be questioned. The United States denied the right of any power, any time, "to visit, molest, or detain" in peacetime an American vessel on the high seas.[25] Polo told the secretary he had received a strictly confidential communication from Madrid offering a new solution. Would it be possible for the United States to make inquiry into the status of the *Virginius* if the ship and men were given up, and (if the result of the investigation required) punish those individuals who had violated laws of the United States, reserving until receipt of further information the Spanish salute to the flag?[26]

Polo's new proposal was interesting. The secretary excused himself and went to another part of the house where President Grant, having just arrived, was conversing with Mrs. Fish and family. He returned with an approval.[27]

It is, incidentally, doubtful that Grant required persuasion. Despite a penchant for reminiscing with old comrades, the President was no jingoist. As his biographer William B. Hesseltine has written, "Even the President might while away a holiday with talk of war and then forget realities, but on the morrow the warrior was a man of peace, supporting the secretary of state in settling problems by diplomacy."[28]

It was agreed, Fish told the admiral, that if Spain made the proposal and surrendered the *Virginius* and its survivors, the salute to the American flag would be postponed until December 25, and if before that date Spain proved the *Virginius* not entitled to carry the American flag the salute would be dispensed with.[29] The admiral wished the secretary the felicitations of the day and withdrew.

Events thus moved so rapidly that the Madrid contestants, Sickles and Carvajal, became bewildered, not only by what their opponents were up to but what their superiors were about. A telegram arrived from Fish to Sickles declaring, "It was supposed here that you had left Madrid inasmuch as you informed me you had then demanded your passports."[30] Sickles on November 29 telegraphed Fish that Carvajal sent "congratulations on this happy termination of the affair." How useless the American minister's excellent diplomacy! The "most eminent jurists of Spain and the European powers" had advised the Madrid administration that public law supported the American claims.[31]

And so at the department on Saturday morning, November 29, Polo and Fish again met and, fresh quills on the desk and ink pots filled, began discussion as to ways to carry out the agreement. For an emergency, that had started with seizure of a ship and the taking of lives, and had evoked such an outcry that two governments' honor seemed to depend on the outcome, it was settled with astonishing ease. If any disagreement arose, Fish did not record it. The protocol was a repetition of what had been discussed in Fish's house two days before. Spain would return the *Virginius* and prisoners to the Americans and agree to salute the American flag on December 25. If Spain proved that the ship was not entitled to fly the flag, the salute would be dispensed with, "but the United States will expect, in such a case, a disclaimer of intent of indignity to its flag in the act which was committed." If either country was wrong, the United States would take action against citizens who had violated its laws, as would Spain those of its authorities who might have infringed laws or treaties. The time, manner, and place of surrender of the ship and survivors was to be decided within the next two days.[32]

The signed agreement was not quite the diplomatic end of the affair, for pressure began to mount on Polo, the admiral feeling nervous about his responsibility. Throughout the crisis he had expressed concern over his inexperience in diplomatic affairs. By December 1, he was beginning to panic because he had not received instructions from Madrid on details of surrender of the *Virginius*. Perhaps he had visions of Sickles shooting the foreign minister in Madrid. Polo sent a note asking for more time to name the date and place of the surrender. He believed the reason he had not received a reply from Madrid was that on Sunday there was no meeting of the Council of State. Aware that this might seem like another evasion, he begged "the honorable secretary of state to extend the time agreed only till the arrival of a telegraphic communication he expects every moment from his government."[33] Fish wrote that he was "instructed by the President to say that the delay appears. . .to have been unavoidable, but the sufficient reasons which have caused it will doubtless cease in a few hours, and the President will then rely upon the immediate execution of the agreement to complete the arrangement of the details for the surrender forthwith of the vessel."[34] The admiral continued to fret over the failure of his government to send directions, and on December 3 came to Fish's house early in the morning, deeply distressed: no cable from Spain. That afternoon he revisited the secretary, and accidentally told Fish he had no authority to arrange the time and place for carrying out the protocol. Fish may have begun to share the admiral's anxiety. That evening, to the secretary's relief, a cable arrived from Sickles. Carvajal had said he was sending instructions to Polo.[35]

CHAPTER EIGHT

The Mechanics of Compromise

O N the evening of December 4, 1873, Secretary of State Fish was working at his desk at home when a servant announced the British minister, Thornton. The latter bustled into the room with a telegram from Britain's consul general at Havana, who, it seemed, had had an interview with Governor General Jovellar and suggested that the *Virginius* might be delivered to him or, as an alternative, sent to Nassau. Jovellar was in favor of this solution. Thornton presented the plan as a man offering two quarrelsome friends a way out. Fish at once said no. The protocol had been drawn up for surrender of the vessel, and anything else would be impractical, if not an insult to American honor.[1] The next day Polo appeared with the same request, contained in a telegram from the Spanish minister to the colonies. Polo left the telegram with the secretary, not returning for an answer until four o'clock that afternoon. Again Fish said no.

The fact that Congress was in session seemed more of a threat than a help to the Grant administration. Senators Simon Cameron of Pennsylvania and Oliver P. Morton of Indiana called at the Department, expressing a wish for amicable settlement but objecting to delivery of the ship to a third party. They thought this might present equal difficulties to Spain. Morton suggested that he introduce a resolution for some accommodation but withdrew the suggestion when his fellow senator and the secretary ruled against him.

The same morning a member of the House of Representatives called on Fish, the graven-faced James A. Garfield of Ohio, who also had the *Virginius* on his mind. He was the bearer of a curious message. It would be better, Garfield warned, for the department to leave the matter until after Congress departed Washington for the Christmas recess. The affair "could be taken care of better if Congress were not around." Fish must have wondered about the worth of an arm of government whose members believed the nation safer when it was not in the capital.[2]

(97)

That afternoon, at the twice-weekly Cabinet meeting, all the secretaries agreed with Fish's decision to decline the Spanish colonial minister's proposition for delivering the *Virginius* to a third party. Secretary Creswell, still advocating a stiff policy, was joined by Robeson in belief that the ship should be delivered to the United States in Cuban waters. The president spoke for his belief that the place of surrender should not stand in the way of a settlement. Grant's voice seemed to counsel peace. But his meandering ideas did an about-face and suggested a policy Fish knew could lead to war. Tell Polo, Grant instructed his secretary of state, that unless the question was adjusted by next Monday he would turn over the matter to Congress. If Fish did not mention the advice of the three congressmen just in his office, it must have come to mind. Were the matter to be turned over to Congress, he told Grant, it would be necessary for the administration to make recommendations. Grant spoke of recognizing the independence of Cuba, a temporary suspension of the Neutrality Act toward the Cuban rebels, and reprisals. If war became inevitable, the United States "should bring about the first blow from Spain." After discussion the president and Cabinet decided not to set any time for the vessel to be delivered but to press for an early decision.[3] The meeting broke up leaving Fish responsible for the successful conclusion of a problem the nation believed settled.

More diplomacy took place with Admiral Polo. That evening Fish sent a note to Polo urging completion of the protocol as to time, place and manner of surrender. A reply came immediately: the admiral had received no authority to deal with the question, but had telegraphed Cuba; Polo pleaded illness and said he would call in the morning.[4] Next morning he was the first visitor to the Department. If he was ill the previous evening, he had received the proper tonic in the form of instructions from Madrid on the manner and time of the *Virginius*'s surrender. With Bancroft Davis recording the conversation, Polo reeled off a set of instructions. Hoisting the United States flag over the vessel must not be mentioned, according to his orders. The Castelar government advised that if they raised the flag it must "not prejudice the rights which Spain might have to the vessel." Fish insisted the flag must be flying at the time of restoration. Polo again asked that mention of the flag be deleted because of the delicate condition of the Spanish government. Fish refused; he was willing, he said, not to make direct mention of the flag, but the flag should be waving when the American navy took over the vessel. He would, he added, be guided by President Grant's wishes, but believed the flag should be flying. Polo left after three hours. Fish and Davis discussed the morning's events before the secretary of state left to attend a Cabinet meeting prior to the admiral's return.

The Cabinet had another long discussion. Fish read an addition to the protocol proposing to settle the question of the flag: if the United States received the *Virginius* with flag flying it would not be prejudicial to the claims of Spain or the United States. Grant assured the Cabinet he would not allow any unimportant point to stand in the way of settlement, but the protocol of November 29 must be followed. Indeed, the President declared, it was not necessary to have the flag flying. Secretaries Robeson and Fish assured him it was necessary for the flag to be raised over the *Virginius*. Grant changed his mind.[5] To the Cabinet it seemed that things had gone well. Public clamor for revenge, which only a few weeks before appeared so threatening, was dying down. Spain was in a conciliatory mood. There had been little trouble from Congress. Grant admitted amazement at the temper of the senators—"he believed if Spain were to send a fleet into the harbor of New York and bombard the city the Senate might pass a resolution of regret that they had had cause for so doing and offer to pay them for the expense of coming over and doing it."[6]

At 2:30, Polo returned to the State Department. The secretary again told him the flag should be flying, and handed the Spaniard his memorandum to the effect that restoration of the vessel with flag flying was not an admission that the ship had the right to fly the flag at the time of its capture nor would it prejudice Spain's right to prove before Christmas that the ship was not entitled to fly the flag when captured. Polo studied the memo for an hour and accepted it. Nevertheless he added that neither should the flag prejudice claims for reparations provided in the protocol. Bancroft Davis combined the two memos, and Polo agreed to the new form. The conference closed.[7]

The admiral was back at the State Department the next day to sign the agreement with Fish naming December 16 for delivery of the *Virginius* at the port of Bahia Honda, about sixty miles west of Havana. According to the admiral's information the ship was in poor condition, leaking and without coal for a voyage to New York.[8] But that was a problem for the American navy.

At the next Cabinet meeting Fish read his agreement with Polo and offered to mention the time and place to anyone who wanted to know. All Cabinet members declined and advised that nothing be said.[9] The same day Bancroft Davis wrote his brother, "We have just gone through the annual Cuban imbroglio—this year growing out of a brutal massacre on the part of the Spaniards, and we managed to get out without being drawn into a war."[10]

The question of insult to the American flag would determine whether further diplomatic maneuvers would be necessary. The matter could only be resolved by finding that the *Virginius* was not a registered American vessel. If fraud was proved in the ship's registration, then it could not claim protection.

The dispute over registration now turned on the findings of an investigation in New York. From November 28 to December 6 men who had commanded or sailed with the *Virginius* came to give testimony at 29 Nassau Street, the office of the U.S. Circuit Court for the southern district of New York. The interrogation was handled by Fish's son-in-law Sidney Webster, attorney for Spain's New York consulate, and by George Bliss as attorney for the United States. The initial witness was Francis Sheppherd, the first captain of the vessel. Sheppherd's testimony alone was enough to show that the sale was fraudulent and the shipowners Cuban. He recounted how he had come to New York to work for the steamship line owned by Marshall O. Roberts. Before taking command of the *Virginius* he had met John F. Patterson who expressed regret at allowing his name to be used in the sale. The transaction was clearly a fraud, not only because Patterson was not the true owner but also because no sureties were ever paid on the vessel as the law required. Captain Sheppherd revealed how the Cuban owners came aboard only after the vessel had cleared New York and of their subsequent involvement in revolutions in both Venezuela and Cuba.[11]

Francis Bowen, who had skippered the *Virginius* in 1872,

succeeded Sheppherd as a witness. Bowen admitted he was offered $5,000 and command of a Cuban privateer if he would land an expedition in Cuba. There was no American flag aboard the ship, according to Bowen.[12]

Captain Charles Smith, Bowen's successor, told the court of trying to bring up Patterson's supposed ownership with the Cubans. The insurgents, according to Smith, would only laugh off the subject saying, "Patterson had got his price; we don't want anything more to do with him."[13]

Testimony by Bowen and Smith showed both complicity and confusion among U.S. consuls toward the ship. The consul at Aspinwall was sympathetic to the Cubans and understood the status of the *Virginius,* yet he had called on the navy to save the ship from Spain's *Pizarro.* Another consul complained to Smith, "The *Virginius* ain't no business to my protection, but I can't help but protect her; I don't know what to do." When an American man-of-war came into the harbor, Smith said, the consul "would try to throw the *Virginius* off on her."[14]

Finally one Adolfo de Varona, a physician practicing in Brooklyn, clinched the case against Patterson's ownership. Three years earlier, de Varona admitted, acting as an agent of the insurrectionists, he gave the money to purchase the *Virginius* to J. K. Roberts. Patterson was present when the money was turned over.[15]

Even before the hearings ended, Attorney Bliss wrote Fish that Patterson was "greatly frightened" and, if the government desired, would give a statement on his connection with the ship, although it might be necessary to grant him freedom from prosecution. Also Ramon Quesada was quoted as saying that the *Virginius* "was bought by subscription among the Cubans and that he controlled her."[16]

The results of the inquiry were all the Spanish consulate in New York and Admiral Polo could have hoped. Polo sent the documents of the *Virginius*'s sale and a summary of the hearing to the secretary of state. At a Cabinet meeting Attorney General Williams informed Grant and Fish that from information gathered both by the government and from Spanish officials it appeared that the vessel belonged to the Junta and not the supposed American owner. Williams suggested that Fish might tell Polo that the right of the *Virginius* to fly the flag was so doubtful that there need be no salute. Grant agreed. Williams advised that in case of a claim by Spain for damages no decision should be given. The Cabinet decided Williams should give a written opinion. If claims were against the United States it would be better to be able to say the vessel had been disclaimed, that the American government had used all diligence in registration, or the United States might be offering the apologies and paying the compensation it now sought from Spain.[17]

Fish soon sent Polo a note about "the satisfaction of the United States that the *Virginius* was not entitled to carry the flag." The government would order the navy at Santiago to dispense with the salute to the flag.[18]

It remained for Attorney General Williams to give a written opinion on the case. Williams was not one to oppose what he felt Grant and the Cabinet wanted to hear but the evidence so clearly indicated doubtful ownership that Williams did not have to stretch his interpretation. The decision nevertheless was a mixture of fact and pretension, legality and bluff. The registration he held "a fraud upon the navigation laws of the United States." Spain, he continued, had no right to seize a vessel on the high seas flying the American flag, for the Madrid government "has no jurisdiction whatever over the question as to whether or not such a vessel is on the high seas in violation of any law of the United States." If Spain could not raise the question of the ship's legality, the United States could, Williams decided, and "without admitting that Spain would otherwise have any interest in the question, I decide that the *Virginius* at the time of her capture was without right and improperly carrying the American flag."[19]

Affairs in Cuba now, at last, began to straighten out. The *New York Times* correspondent in Havana reported that the city appeared to be quieting down. The Casino Español was having second thoughts and local Spaniards beginning to favor a quiet settlement rather than a course which would place them in rebellion against Spain. To Consul Henry Hall it seemed that Captain General Jovellar "was equal to the emergency."[20] The Cuban press was beginning to soften its editorials, a result of pressure by Jovellar. The captain general was still the representative of Spain, and regardless of what contempt Peninsulars had for the republic they recognized the necessity of obeying Spanish authority.[21]

(102)

Jovellar at last carried out the terms of the *Virginius* agreement negotiated in Washington. He assured Hall he would adhere to the terms, but at first asked if they could be modified. Hall apparently agreed, as he pointed out to Bancroft Davis that "it would probably make the situation of our people less disagreeable than at present and facilitate the pacific settlement of other matters pending. Otherwise I would advise no concession whatever."[22] Two days afterward, on December 11, Jovellar issued a proclamation both to explain his actions and prepare for the surrender. He had done everything possible, the proclamation read, to work for a favorable solution. It now was his duty to obey orders. "Want of compliance therewith would bring on war, war with a great power and war without the aid of Spain, today more than ever torn by fratricidal and intestine strife."[23]

The American community in Havana still believed the pro-Spanish Cubans to be dangerous, but in fact the crisis was over. For a Spaniard standing on the waterfront watching a group of laborers from the Spanish arsenal busy filling the hold of the *Virginius* with ballast, the issue was clear. They were readying the ship for sea, for surrender to the Americans, who doubtless once more would send it against the loyalists of Cuba. Feeling of sorrow mingled with the simple desire to get even with somebody. Few signs of life were in evidence around the ship on Thursday, December 11, save for small boats moving in the harbor. That evening Spanish authorities notified the Havana Tugboat Company to have a tug ready at three the following morning.

On Friday, December 12, 1873, at 4:00 A.M., Santiago's harbor showed no bustle, ships large and small lying in the calm water, silence broken by bells clanging the time. The tug *Indio*'s engines violated the silence as the little boat maneuvered into position alongside the *Virginius*. Slowly it pushed and coaxed its large companion in the direction of the *Isabel de Catolica*, which was to lead the *Virginius* to Bahia Honda. Opposite the *Isabel* the tug slacked and for a few minutes the three vessels remained almost stationary. The Spanish frigate's ponderous wheels began to revolve. In a few minutes the little flotilla was opposite the office of the captain of the port. A sleepy

(103)

customhouse officer turned to an American correspondent watching the scene and remarked, either from ignorance or irony, "I wonder what gunboats those are going out so early in the morning?" A few more minutes and the three vessels had passed the mouth of the harbor and were beyond the guns of Morro Castle. No further sound was heard.

As day started to break the tug *Indio* came chugging back into harbor alone. A sentry, walking the ramparts of the Morro, impatiently awaiting relief, if he looked out to sea could have seen the *Isabel* and *Virginius* moving in a westerly direction.[24]

News of the sailing reached Havana later that day. The men in the Casino Español (Spanish Club) grew angry. Over glasses in the cafes and cigars in private houses, men shook their heads. A circular addressed "To the Spanish People" condemned the surrender and damned the Castelar republic.[25] That night a mob of several hundred men went into Campo de Marto Square and then to the Plaza de Armas where they gathered in front of the palace of the captain general. Shots were fired, but the mob proved indecisive, possibly frightened. No leaders came forward, though the men stayed before the palace until midnight when Jovellar appeared, perhaps not so much out of fear as because it was impossible to sleep. He addressed the men. They dispersed. It was the last convulsion of defiance from the Peninsulars.[26]

The question of saluting the American flag remained. In Santiago harbor Captain R.B. Lowry of the *Kansas* sent a copy of the protocol terms to General Burriel and reminded him of orders to receive a twenty-one-gun salute on December 25, which he would return "gun for gun."[27] Burriel wrote back that Lowry need not have taken the trouble to inform him as his superior had furnished him with a copy. Because Lowry's copy had no seal or signature it lacked, said Burriel, the "condition of its legal or official character."[28] The salute would be fired, and Burriel named the place, Morro Castle, three and a half miles away. Lowry answered in amazement at the choice of a battery "out of sight from my vessel from which to give and receive the salutes with which we are charged." He knew international salutes had always been done from Battery Blanco in the harbor, and it would be "inconvenient and impossible," he told Burriel, to leave anchorage to receive the salute at the harbor entrance.[29] Burriel came back testily with an explanation that the battery where salutes were formerly given was under repair. If Lowry did not accept the Morro, he would suspend orders.[30]

Again it seemed the work of diplomacy was in danger of being lost by a quarrel between two lesser officials. What the outcome might have been had Burriel and Lowry continued is hard to say, for demands to salute the flag were serious matters in nineteenth century diplomatic and military policy. If the United States had insisted and Burriel continued to refuse, trouble might have ensued. Fortunately, about this time it was decided in Washington that because of the dubious character of the *Virginius* the United States government would dispense with the salute. Lowry could write to Burriel with satisfaction, "I have no further business with your excellency in this matter. I now bid you farewell."[31]

Meanwhile, after a month in jail the survivors in Santiago by early December were beginning to think those men who went to the wall had been the fortunates. Spain's prisons had never been noted for humanity, and treatment of insurgents and pirates could be harsh. Jailors used clubs freely, and it seemed to an American Civil War veteran from Harrisburg, Simon Gratz, that they used them most frequently on British subjects who were black West Indians. The prisoners felt a surge of hope when American naval officers appeared to dispense the food, money and tobacco, but when the officers left life returned to the same dirty and foul-smelling routine.

Then, at 4:00 A.M., December 3, occurred a change in the jail routine. Henry Canals awakened from his fitful sleep to the cursing and kicks of jailors in the large room that held the prisoners. Lights from lanterns flickered on tumbling bodies, and men exhausted mentally, in a way sleep could not heal, rubbed their eyes and looked about. Canals felt his arms being roughly bound as he and his companions marched out of jail to the street down which Ryan, Fry and others had taken their last walk. The direction was not the slaughter house, but the Morro Castle six miles away.[32] The Morro Castles of Santiago and Havana were to Cuban insurgents as much symbols of tyranny as the Bastille had been of repression in France.

(105)

The place of incarceration had been changed. Into the centuries-old fort at Santiago the ragged men limped. Guards herded the prisoners into a single room about twenty yards long and only four or five wide. Throughout that December day the men found these quarters almost intolerable, no space to lie or sit.

There followed another change. At midnight a jailor appeared at the door, shouting at them to prepare to go to sea. Stories of prisoners being dropped through trap doors to the shark-infested water below must have been in the minds of many as they were again shoved out the door and into a courtyard. A heavy guard formed around the prisoners as the gates of the castle opened. With guns of the guards at the ready, a quick step was called off, and the rows of men marched down the heights from the castle toward water's edge, almost like lemmings drawn back toward the sea from whence they had come.[33]

The entire body of prisoners thereupon boarded the Spanish gunboat *Bazan* where their captors continued to badger them with reports they were on their way to execution. Destination was Havana, they claimed, where Volunteers would make short work of the job. Arms badly swollen from the tight bonds, the prisoners found themselves penned in a hold, dark as a dungeon, damp, unbelievably filthy, with a pack of mules penned on the deck above, animal wastes streaming down through fissures in the deck into the pesthole, the men helpless and the guards taunting them. "Now you rebel dogs see what the American government will do for you." Water was served in buckets from which Canals claimed the mules had drunk.

At this point there was a change for the better. The men never reached Havana, for Consul General Hall was demanding of the captain general that the men return to Santiago. Jovellar relented. When they reached Santiago the men were transferred into the Morro again.[34]

The prisoners were handed over to Captain D. L. Braine of the *Juniata* on December 18, and he and his staff set about to relieve their physical condition and rags. The *New York Times* had reported that "treatment of the prisoners was not harsh by Spanish standards," and in some respects this was right, but the prisoners told of beatings and their condition supported their claims.[35]

In contrast to the dozens of compatriots the American public had believed to be languishing in Cuban jails, only thirteen among the ninety-one of the *Virginius*'s survivors claimed United States citizenship. One individual from the island of St. Thomas believed he was a British subject. Authorities dryly informed him St. Thomas was a Danish possession.[36] From the Spanish names of some of the men it was obvious that at best they were naturalized citizens and more likely of double citizenship. Charles A. Knight, it was noted, who claimed to be from New York, spoke English with an accent and was fluent in Spanish.

All survivors, regardless of citizenship, elected to go to New York aboard the *Juniata*.[37] There the men were turned over to the care of Los Amigos de Cuba until provision could be made for sending them to their various homes. It was reported that they breakfasted in José Trujillo's restaurant at 76 Pine Street. At noon Trujillo called the group to order, and it was agreed that they would present Sir Lambton Lorraine with a sword. The men regarded Commander Braine of the *Juniata* as nearly as great a benefactor as the British captain, and when they learned that Braine's youngest child had died before their arrival in port they went as a group to the funeral.

Soon afterward stories began to appear relating that the Junta had given an ungenerous welcome to the men. They were not treated to a meal at Trujillo's, one survivor reported. The Junta said it would no longer be responsible for them. The men wished they had stayed aboard the *Juniata*. With charges and countercharges of ungraciousness the men of the *Virginius* dropped from sight, and from the pages of history.[38]

CHAPTER NINE

Burial at Sea

THE *Despatch,* carrying the chief of staff of the North Atlantic squadron, Captain W. D. Whiting, left Key West on Sunday, December 16, 1873, at 10:00 A.M., and twenty-four hours later the blue-green hills of Cuba appeared in the distance. Soon the *Despatch* was standing off an old yellow fort called Murrilo which commanded the entrance to the harbor of Bahia Honda, now clearly in view. The day was misty. Reducing speed, the ship crept toward a narrow but clearly marked channel leading to smooth water where the *Virginius* was expected to be anchored.[1]

When the American vessel came into view, notwithstanding a Republican edict to the contrary, the harbor guard ran up a Spanish monarchical flag. As that outlawed banner unfurled in the morning breeze the Americans could see a black sidewheel steamship with two smokestacks about a mile beyond the fort lying in perfectly smooth water.

Lieutenant Commander Rodgers, captain of the *Despatch,* proceeded slowly, refusing assistance of two Cuban pilots. After more than an hour of maneuvering the Americans dropped anchor in seven-and-a-half fathoms, about four hundred yards from the *Virginius.* No craft other than two coastal schooners were visible. Not until anchored did the Americans observe a Spanish sloop-of-war close under the shore about two-and-a-half miles away.

With the Americans anchored, a boat pulled away from the sloop and eventually moved alongside the *Virginius.* At 2:15 P.M. the American flag, raised by Spanish seamen, floated once more over the renegade vessel, and the Spanish boat pushed off.

Scanning the distant sloop through glasses for any chance of treachery, the Americans saw another boat let down from the Spanish vessel which turned out to be the captain's gig. A few minutes' hard rowing by the gig's seamen brought the

Spaniards, in the person of a handsome officer in full uniform, to the *Despatch*. Commander Rodgers met his visitor at the gangway. The Spaniard introduced himself as Commander Manuel de la Cámara, of the sloop-of-war *Favorita*. For several months, Cámara told the American, he had been surveying in the vicinity. He was now ordered to supervise return of the *Virginius*. Rodgers offered Cámara the courtesies of naval tradition and invited him to his cabin, but Cámara, informed that Whiting was there to receive the *Virginius*'s surrender, stepped up to him, and both men raised their caps in solemn salute. Cámara advised Whiting that he had a copy of the protocol agreed to by their nations and was ready to put it into effect either that day or Tuesday. Whiting pointed out that his orders were to receive the vessel on Tuesday, but he would leave the hour of delivery to the Spaniard. After quick consultation the officers agreed to deliver the vessel at nine o'clock the next morning. Whiting asked how much coal the *Virginius* had on board and was told enough for six days. Again salutes. Cámara climbed down to his waiting gig. Only five minutes had passed since the Spaniard first had come on board.[2]

Later that afternoon Captain Whiting and a junior officer returned the call. The Spanish officers received them pleasantly, but conversation confined itself to commonplace topics and remarks about the harbor and surrounding country. Courtesies fulfilled, the Americans returned to their ship.

Tuesday dawned bright and clear, and the mist which the previous day had hung about the coast and almost hidden the Spanish vessel lifted early to reveal a beautiful landscape. The only spectators to the little drama being acted out in Bahia Honda were a few fishermen. Some Americans had chartered a vessel and presented themselves at the harbor entrance, but the authorities turned them back for lack of credentials. After several attempts to enter, they sailed away.[3]

All eyes looked toward the Spanish ship. At 8:30 A.M. the gig from the *Favorita* containing oarsmen and one officer came alongside the *Virginius*. The officer stepped on deck and sent the petty officer and a half-dozen men, who had stood watch on the *Virginius* during the night, over the side into the steamer's dinghy.

The American ship waited. The men aboard the *Despatch*

knew of the executions six weeks before and had read or heard of the clamor for war. Perhaps some knew of the diplomatic efforts to avoid bloodshed. Many probably were among those who had hoped that war would come.

Exactly at nine o'clock the American flag once again unfurled above the *Virginius* and Whiting and his assistant, Lieutenant Marix, put away from the *Despatch*. When they reached the *Virginius* the lone figure of Cámara stood ready to receive them on deck. Again the officers, who might have been exchanging broadsides instead of salutes if diplomacy had failed, greeted each other. In obedience to his government's requirement, Cámara said, he had the honor to turn over the steamer *Virginius*. Another word or two, and in ten minutes the Spaniard was back on his own deck.[4]

The *Virginius* was under American command. A prize crew under Chief Engineer Harris made a survey and found that the engines were extremely dirty but otherwise seemingly in working order. The ship as a whole was filthy. The Spaniards apparently had decided that while the Americans might recover the ship it would not be a clean one. Everything that was movable appeared to have been taken except for a half-dozen casks of water and "a few vermin which haunted the mattresses and cushions in the cabin." A foul stench came from the forecastle and below the hatches. Decks were caked with dirt and excrement, mold and decomposition. As the men wandered over the ship looking for trophies they turned up only a bayonet, drill, and chart. The latter was of the Windward passages in the neighborhood of Cuba, Jamaica, and Haiti with annotations and marks of a course thought to have been that of the *Virginius*, so it was preserved on the possibility it might be useful.[5] At the stern two brass swivel guns, with the name *Virginius* stamped on them, had hung impotently in place through another change of ownership.

The officers aboard were reluctant to put American seamen in the filthy forecastle and ended up stowing them away in the hardly cleaner quarters offered by the staterooms of Ryan and companions.

At two o'clock the *Virginius*, with fires lit, steamed for two hundred yards before its engines suddenly stopped. The *Despatch* came alongside, attached a tow line, and ignominiously

(111)

hauled the former blockade-runner out of the harbor, past the fort with its royal flag flapping defiantly. In an hour the two ships were at sea.

After several hours the American tug *Fortune* came up at 8:00 P.M. and stayed with the convoy for the night. In the meantime Lieutenant Marix and Engineers Calhoun and Lamdin again got the engines of the *Virginius* going.[6] Fortunately the sea was calm as a millpond. At eight o'clock, Wednesday morning, a consultation was held, and the *Despatch* stopped towing the *Virginius*. The *Fortune* left to report to Rear Admiral G. H. Scott, commander of the North Atlantic squadron, at Key West. The *Despatch* and *Virginius* continued to steam to Dry Tortugas where a coal schooner was standing by, together with the sloop-of-war *Ossipee*, ordered to accompany the *Virginius* on the voyage to New York.[7]

At the Dry Tortugas, in Florida, Midshipmen E. B. Underwood and F. A. Tyler aboard the *Ossipee*, tasting their first sea life after graduating from the Naval Academy the previous spring, awaited duty, and their hearts must have sunk when they were chosen to be part of the prize crew for the *Virginius* under Lieutenant Commander D. C. Woodrow. Underwood found the *Virginius* in terrible shape, leaking badly, "her hatches gone, furniture broken and damaged, clocks and gauges taken down, gutted of their works, then filled with unmentionable filth and returned to their places." Worst of all was that the ship was "alive with cockroaches—the large tropic kind, the kind that fly at night and can be heard to bring up with a thud against a bulkhead."[8]

When work parties tried to patch the ship they found two defects which they could not remedy—the boilers that had suffered in the desperate attempt to escape from the *Tornado*, and a leak in the port bow which kept the forward compartment about a third full of water which there was no way to pump out.

Encountering these conditions, Underwood and his friend Tyler also felt the beginnings of a rough sea which soon broke into their transom quarters and chased them wet and shivering with their soaked mattresses to a cabin floor. As the little convoy sailed north, the sea rose. Rivets of one of the bow plates came loose and leaked so badly that limber holes in the forward bulkhead had to be plugged to keep the fire room clear. The

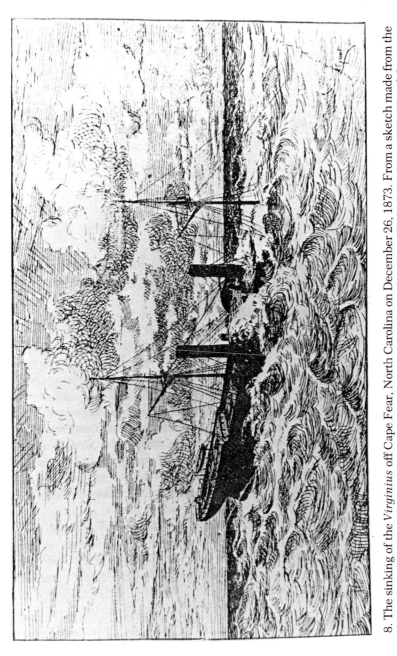

8. The sinking of the *Virginius* off Cape Fear, North Carolina on December 26, 1873. From a sketch made from the deck of the U.S.S. *Ossipee* by Lieutenant Commander Gouv. K. Haswell, U.S.N. From *U.S. Naval Institute Proceedings* 51 (1925).

crew increased its efforts to help the low-listing ship continue the voyage. To lighten the vessel the port anchor and other bulky material was thrown overboard. The next day there nevertheless was nine to ten feet of water in the forward compartment whose bulkhead seemed to young Underwood to protrude "like the stomach of a high-liver." Props of timber were fashioned, and the crew wedged these against the bulkhead to relieve pressure. It was obvious that it might give way, and water then would rush aft to put out the boiler fires.

On the twenty-fourth the wind picked up, the *Virginius* signaled the *Ossipee* that the ship's condition had become dangerous, and the two vessels headed toward shore.

Christmas day was a dreary affair, particularly for Underwood and Tyler spending their first Christmas away from home. Clothing and bedding were drenched, nothing but cold food available. In spite of the pumps the water continued to rise.

At 4:00 A. M. on the twenty-sixth the last boiler gave out, cutting off power to the pumps. Water in the engine room flooded the fires. At last Commander Woodrow gave orders to signal the *Ossipee* to take the men off. At daylight the tow line was shortened to one hundred feet and a cutter began making the passage between the two ships, seas running high. Five trips were necessary before all men were safely back on the *Ossipee*. No time could be wasted on equipment, so they left all their personal effects. Aboard the *Ossipee*, Underwood went below to get dry clothes and warm food and some decent sleep.

The *Virginius* was in no rush to go to her doom. Neither in life nor in death could the craft seem to make much speed. When Underwood came back on deck he realized the end was near, for the tow line between the two ships had been cut and a buoy made fast to its end.

At 4:17 in the afternoon of December 26, 1873, stern high in the air, the *Virginius* plunged beneath the Atlantic. As water reached the cabin, the poop deck burst with a loud explosion, and the ship sank rapidly. Underwood felt a surge of exultation watching it go down, knowing that the "colony of cockroaches had at last got its 'come uppance'."

At five o'clock, with a terrific gale blowing up, the *Ossipee* got under way for New York. To its stern a buoy danced crazily on the waves, its bell tolling a warning to all seamen.

(114)

CHAPTER TEN

Aftermath

O N December 8, while Fish and Polo were debating whether the *Virginius* should be surrendered with a bare flagstaff, Benjamin Moran entered in his journal, "News has reached London that General Sickles has resigned his post at Madrid. This is no doubt true, and the step has probably grown out of the fact that Mr. Fish has taken the *Virginius* negotiations out of the general's hand and is conducting them over his head at Washington."[1] Moran's information was partly correct, for two days earlier Sickles had telegraphed Fish, "It is published semiofficially that the government disapproves of my conduct in the case of the *Virginius*." If, in Grant's opinion, his resignation would be in the public interest, "such resignation may be considered as hereby respectfully tendered."[2]

The reason why Sickles now chose to resign lay not so much in attacks of the Spanish press as in his pride. The Madrid newspapers had shown an understandable hostility toward him before and he had brushed it aside, but if Moran could read enough from cables to understand Sickles had been supplanted as diplomatic agent of his government others could do so.[3] Instead of bringing the negotiation through to a triumphant conclusion over a humbled Spain, or by occupying a dramatic position at the beginning of a grand Spanish-American war, Sickles suspected he might be in the position of an army officer stripped of his command for incompetence. Nothing so melodramatic had occurred as to make him a spectacle of ridicule, no epaulets torn from his shoulder, no saber broken over Fish's knee, yet Sickles resented what he considered an affront.[4] He declared to Layard that Fish's procedure was "totally inadequate," and would not be accepted by American public opinion.[5] Thinking that if he returned to the United States he could stir up trouble against the settlement, Sickles offered his resignation.[6] In a showdown between himself and Fish, his friend Grant perhaps would choose him. The general was dis-

FISH VS. SICKLES

John Bull to Spain: "It's difficult Fishing here!"

(Nast in *Harper's Weekly*)

9. A Thomas Nast cartoon of the contretemps between Fish and Sickles. The scroll Fish is lunging for reads "Resignation of Dan Sickles." From *Harper's Weekly*, November 29, 1873.

appointed, for Fish had cabled back immediately, "No dissatisfaction has been expressed . . . and it is deemed important that
you remain. Your resignation at this time would not be accepted, as it would interfere with prospects of an accommodation."[7] Sickles fumed. As his biographer has written, "If there
was anything he could not stomach it was derision."[8] And
Sickles was an object of scorn in Madrid.

In subsequent weeks Sickles would continue to meet frustra-
tion, for with the exception of his friends in the *New York
Herald* the country made no protest against the settlement.[9]
There was a feeling of relief that the nation had escaped war. As
for reparations, it seemed to Sir Edward Thornton that Americans felt they had "obtained quite as much as they had a right to
expect whilst a minority believes that the demands were exag-
gerated and even harsh."[10]

Sickles again wrote on December 4, this time requesting that
the telegram tendering his resignation, together with Fish's
reply, be published.[11] Fish was anxious to be rid of the general
but as at that time the *Virginius* had not yet been delivered it
was possible the affair was not settled and it would be inconvenient to have Sickles resign. The secretary told Sickles that
since his tender of resignation was only hypothetical and he had
referred to unknown publications, and no dissatisfaction was
expressed, publication of the correspondence was "not necessary and could not be authorized."[12]

Sickles on December 20 offered his resignation for the third
time and that was too much.[13] By now Spain had surrendered
the *Virginius* and crew. Sickles, Fish told Thornton, was showing a spirit hostile to the administration by sending newspaper
communications "devoid of truth." Grant told Fish it was up to
him whether to accept Sickles's resignation but said not to
entrust the general with any details of reparations.[14] Fish now
lost no time in ending Sickles's official stay in Madrid.

Even before the secretary of state had agreed to the resignation, American newspapers and journals were in favor of turning Sickles out, and there was no protest. The *New York Times*
ungraciously said "good riddance."[15] *The Nation* snapped, "He
has never been anything but a disgrace to us all."[16] The only
concern was that Grant might appoint someone worse. According to the *New York Tribune*, "The country is always a little

anxious when an important place falls to the disposition of the President. . .he does not shine in his civil service appointments, and it is hardly to be expected that he will make an appointment for Spain which shall be an improvement upon General Sickles."[17]

This was not the end of Sickles, who remained in the Madrid legation until his letter of recall arrived by steamer mail. He continued to send the Department his dispatches on Spanish affairs and bombarded Fish with requests for publication of his telegrams submitting his resignations and Fish's replies. In his own mind the general had become a martyr to the plots of the secretary of state, and apparently believed that publication would not only vindicate him but unmask Fish. Relying on Grant's friendship he begged "that this request may be submitted to the President."[18] Angered at the manner in which he believed the minister to France, Elihu Washburne, had undermined his position, he complained that the Spanish government's organ, *La Discusion*, had announced that Washburne had sent Castelar data showing the American press favorable to the Spanish republic. This, said Sickles, was the third time Washburne had interfered. Fish should tell Washburne "to confine himself to his prescribed duties."[19]

Events of more importance than the general's irritations were to intrude upon the peace of the Spanish capital, for another act in the latter nineteenth century tragedy known as Spanish politics was about to be played in Madrid. When the Cortes had invested President Castelar with dictatorial powers in September, 1873, it adjourned until the following January. With the day of reassembly approaching, Castelar's opponents amassed arguments in favor of removing him. They could point to the insurgents still in Cartagena defying the republic, to Carlist armies threatening Bilbao in the north, and could argue that Castelar had given in to the United States over the *Virginius*. Castelar's party was as divided as ever. It seemed certain that he would fall, the result being a revival of federalism.[20]

For many Spaniards federalism was synonymous with anarchy, and this view proved decisive, for it was the view of the captain general of Madrid, General Don Manuel Pavia, a soldier who was a supporter of Castelar. Fearful of what new trouble might befall if the government did not maintain its power in the coming legislative session, Pavia urged Castelar to dissolve the assembly or postpone it, and promised to use troops to suppress disorder. The president, driven beyond the limits of his conscience to save the Spanish state, refused to go further to save his administration.[21]

The day for reassembly of the Cortes, January 2, 1874, found the session beginning at 2:00 P.M. On the blue bench of the ministry the entire Cabinet had turned out to support their chief, with the exception of the minister of colonies who was in Cuba. Castelar began with one of his trademark orations, but instead of a spellbinding performance the chief executive read his message arguing that the republic had used its unlimited powers in a careful, effective way. He mentioned his success in the *Virginius* affair. His government had settled it without more war and "sustained principles of international law."[22] It was a plea for the life of the republic. "We must close forever the era of popular risings and military pronouncements."[23] With the end of his speech, debate began on a vote of confidence. At seven that evening the debate was adjourned for dinner. When discussion resumed at 11:00 P.M., Castelar again defended himself. He preferred, he told the Cortes, "the worst republic to the best monarchy."[24]

Alas, it was the end. Even as Castelar spoke, the soldiers of Pavia were surrounding the Cortes. The President could count only on his supporters; he had won no converts. When the final speech had been delivered, the last defense made, the vote was taken early in the morning of January 3, and Castelar lost. Left and center had combined, 120-100. Castelar rose with dignity, resigned, and asked that for the welfare of the country a new government be formed.

It was easier to dissolve a government than to form one, and the opposition could not agree on a successor, and at this point Pavia intervened. He had kept himself informed of what the deputies were doing, and when news came that Castelar was defeated the general called out his troops and occupied all streets leading to the House of Deputies. To Pavia the fall of Castelar meant the beginning of anarchy. At dawn, a misty winter morning, two of his aides came into the Cortes. Courteously but firmly they told the president of the chamber that they had the "painful obligation of requesting that he tell the de-

puties to leave the building." Many deputies, summoning up
bravado, claimed they would rather die in their seats than see
Spain fall victim to another coup. They applauded the minister
of war, Sanchez Brequa, who said he would issue a decree
depriving General Pavia of all honors and decorations.

At this juncture everything played into Pavia's hands. In a
volte-face from the previous night's work the assembly prepared a resolution of confidence in Castelar. It would have
passed unanimously, but Castelar would lack power and not be
obeyed, and the philosopher-statesman was unwilling to return
to power by an act of violence. A message of the deputies'
repentance and willingness to return Castelar to power was
sent to Pavia, who shook his head sadly and said, "Ya es tarde"
("It is too late now"). Soldiers advanced on the chamber, a few
shots were fired in the air, the deputies cleared the hall. No
Spanish Roland remained to contest the ground. According to
the official report it was 6:30 A.M., January 3, 1874.[25] It was at
this time that three of Castelar's friends found the ex-president
sitting in a chair in the chamber, violently ill, murmuring
incoherent phrases. They took him to his house where his
condition for some time was described as critical.

Castelar's departure from office, predicted for weeks, came as
a relief to the Spanish public. People closed their shops and
filled the streets as if it were a holiday.[26] With the end of his
turbulent administration Castelar went back to his lectures as
professor of history at the University of Madrid.

As for the new government, Pavia was no reactionary but his
coup marked a return to the theory that in times of dissolution
and crises, the army represented the national will.[27] The republic remained only in name.

Two days after the end of Castelar's ministry, the distinguished American lawyer, Caleb Cushing, in far-off Massachusetts sat down to write a friend of his feelings on the
Virginius affair. The United States was lucky, he declared, that
it had Castelar to deal with in the crisis. A different Spanish
executive might have meant war. Unlike most of the American
people, Cushing realized that while danger had passed, conditions which created a threat to peace were unchanged—"The
question of Cuba still remains, palpitating, to be settled, no one
knows how, perhaps by some unforeseen accident."[28]

(120)

10. Caleb Cushing, who succeeded Daniel Sickles as minister to Spain. From *Dictionary of American Portraits* (New York: Dover Publications, 1967).

From the beginning, Cushing had taken keen interest in the *Virginius* dispute, although it was no more than one would expect from a man who loved Spain and was a well-known lawyer; but he was now taking an even closer look, as he expected to be representing his country in Spain. Secretary Fish had suggested Cushing as Sickles's replacement. "He is a thorough Spanish scholar," Fish wrote Grant, "and I think his appointment will give more confidence to the country, and will be more likely to result in satisfactory decisions than that of any other man."[29] Critics could point out that Cushing had been accused of sympathizing with Spain because on several occasions he had served as an attorney for the Madrid government, but he was eminently qualified for a diplomatic mission.

His background was remarkable. He had traveled in Spain almost forty years earlier, familiarizing himself with its customs, and with the people for whom he developed admiration. Like Sickles he could speak fluent Spanish—as well as French, German, Italian, and a little Chinese. His diplomatic experience dated to the early 1840s when he had journeyed to China to conclude a treaty with the Middle Kingdom. As a leading member of the American bar his most recent triumph had been arguing his country's case in the *Alabama* claims. Seventy-three-years old in 1874, he astonished strangers when they learned his age, for he both looked and acted years younger. He seemed a man for all posts and seasons.

To appoint so able an individual would not prove easy for the Grant administration and there followed a bewildering series of moves by which Grant decided to offer Cushing a seat on the Supreme Court only to withdraw his name in the face of Senate opposition, whereupon Congressional opponents made no objection to his becoming minister to Spain.[30] On February 8, 1874, Cushing received instructions from the secretary of state as envoy extraordinary and minister plenipotentiary at a generous allowance of $12,000 a year. If not the greatest honor to cap an illustrious career, the post was important at the moment, and Cushing possessed a New England conscience concerning duty.[31]

No illusion could have been in his mind on the wintry March day when his ship put to sea. The *Virginius* case was past the point where it would lead to war, but bargaining remained and, as Cushing had expressed it, the question of Cuba was still palpitating. Friends in Cuba had apprised him of island news. In Havana the Casino again was in control. With news of appointment of a new captain general reaching the island, the Volunteers threatened to revolt. The island was in the throes of an inflation of paper money and "as soon as the soldiers discover that the paper in which they are paid is worthless," so one of Cushing's informants hoped, "their patriotism will be very lukewarm."[32]

The minister disembarked from the *St. Laurent* at Le Havre in good order, and in Paris met the ex-minister, Sickles, who was not stingy with advice.[33] How much of this was based on observation, how much on pride, is impossible to know, but Cushing was the man to take the general's measure. He was not going to Spain expecting miracles. In spite of sympathy for Castelar and republicanism he recognized the republic's frailty. Political change introduced by military usurpation, he wrote Fish, was accepted in Spain. Ironically, even Castelar, so he noted, had said that each of the great steps in the political liberalization of modern Spain had been due to political revolution begun by generals.[34] Cushing reached Madrid the last day of May, 1874, two and a half months after leaving the United States. He met the new President of Spain, Marshal Serrano, who held dictatorial powers, and then waited until June 26 to present American claims to the minister of state, Augusto Ulloa.[35]

Two problems remained with regard to the *Virginius* affair. First, the matter of reparations to families of victims. Second, the more difficult question of punishment for those officials responsible for the executions, in particular General Juan D. Burriel.

The new minister had arrived in Spain at the beginning of summer, a fortunate time according to Layard, for "revolutions and ministerial crises rarely occur in Spain in the summer. The heat is too great for violent enterprise."[36] Cushing lost no time making himself agreeable to the government to which he was accredited and soon the Spaniards appreciated his ability.[37] The reparations issue moved toward settlement. By July, 1874, soon after becoming acquainted with the minister of state, Cushing told Fish he did not expect trouble in settling the claims.[38] The

(123)

key turned out to be that the Spanish government had made a cash settlement for damages to British citizens without specifying they were for the *Virginius,* adopting this tactic to prevent argument by the United States that the government in Madrid was admitting liability. Ulloa had confessed to Layard that because Castelar had negotiated mainly in private, leaving the Foreign Office with few records, the government did not know what the United States would demand or what had been promised.[39] He was afraid the Americans might take advantage of any concessions to Britain as a precedent for claims which Serrano's government would not admit.[40] On August 10, Spain agreed to pay £300 for each black person and £500 for each white, for a total of £7,700, but while American claims were pending the Serrano regime would not admit the principle involved.[41]

Cushing kept a close watch on the Anglo-Spanish talks over reparations. Four months passed between the initial Spanish promise to pay Britain and the actual payment, with Spain in the meantime attempting to conceal the arrangement from the United States. Admiral Polo played this game in Washington, and it was continued by Spain's new minister, a lawyer with liberal credentials, Antonio Mantilla, whom the government sent on July 1. It was not a well-kept secret, for Fish began hearing rumors in October that Spain had paid Britain, and cabled Cushing for information.[42] When Cushing questioned his now fast friend Layard, the Englishman could see no point in keeping the settlement a secret.[43]

Shortly the Spanish minister in Washington paid a call on Fish to ask somewhat sheepishly if the United States would agree to the same settlement as had the British. Some of the differences, he supposed, would have to be turned over to arbitration. Fish agreed, adding that the British had made a distinction between white and black subjects which the United States could not allow.[44] At the Cabinet meeting next day Grant authorized Fish's proposal to demand $2,500 for each American citizen shot. Secretary Robeson wanted a higher sum, but Fish pointed out that $2,500 per person was more than the British received. Besides, Fish coolly added, he did not want to claim too high an indemnity for filibusters.[45] At his meeting with Mantilla, Fish told the Spaniard that Cushing had initiated

(124)

the indemnity negotiations in Madrid and it seemed appropriate to end them there. It would be necessary to conclude the talks before Congress met, so the President could announce it in his message. This would have a "quieting effect." In a cordial mood Mantilla assented.[46]

The end of this problem was in sight. Fish cabled Cushing on November 28, 1874 that the arrangements made in Madrid were acceptable, and instructed Cushing that all of the crew not claimed by Britain must be treated as American seamen. Families of Captain Fry, the mate, engineers, purser, and doctor should have more. Cushing also was to ask indemnity for detention and imprisonment of American citizens not executed.[47]

As so often happened when a Spanish government was on the verge of making a settlement with the United States, another change of government occurred. On December 28, 1874, the republic expired when the army made a *pronunciamiento* in favor of the seventeen-year-old Alfonso, heir to the throne and son of Isabel II whose fall in 1868 had ushered in this tragic era for the nation. On January 11, 1875, Cushing was a fascinated spectator as the young monarch, after arriving in nineteenth-century luxury at the train station, rode a white horse like one of his sixteenth century predecessors to attend the singing of a *Te Deum* at the cathedral. Alfonso continued down the principal avenues, Callo de Alcala, Puerto del Sol and Calle Major, and was welcomed at the palace where in the throne room he met the country's grandees and dignitaries. To Cushing the king looked younger than seventeen, but bore himself well, and the immense crowds watching the procession were well behaved.[48]

Five days later the American minister had his first interview with the new minister of state, Castro, and after the usual expressions of good will lost no time in getting to business. "The object of the interview," he said, "is to resume negotiations on the *Virginius*." The Spaniard agreed. "President Grant," Cushing continued, "has led the United States Congress to believe at the beginning of this session that the problems between us were close to settlement. Now only six weeks remain, and we would like to have it settled before Congress adjourns." Cushing urged Castro to compare the trifling cost of settlement with the cost of a single year of war. Castro appeared "visibly affected" and promised to take up the matter at once.[49] The American pressed the point that the United States should get more in indemnities than Britain because most of the British subjects were laborers while the Americans were officers.[50]

Unlike other occasions when American diplomats had been obliged to begin again, Cushing in 1875 found the monarchy ready to continue negotiations where the previous administration had left off. In this sense the monarchy seemed an improvement. In an interview between Cushing and Castro the latter went so far as to declare that the proceedings at Santiago in 1873 were indefensible and required indemnification. He claimed, probably truthfully, to have said so at the time to Castelar, as did the new president of the council.[51]

By early February, 1875, two weeks after the beginning of the monarchy, Cushing could report that the indemnity problem was substantially settled by an exchange of notes "which guard all our own pretensions whether of fact or doctrine." The Spaniards' payment to Britain had required the latter to account for distribution to the United States, while Cushing suggested no such accounting.[52]

The minister drew up a final proposal in which the United States would accept $80,000 in full satisfaction of the claims. The compact was unconditional, the money to be distributed among injured parties without accountability to Spain. Next day Cushing called on Castro and was told Spain was ready to sign. It remained for Cushing to be presented to King Alfonso and accord his government recognition. When making a presentation speech to the king, Cushing told Castro he would refer to "the king's great ancestor, Charles III, who made the first treaty with the United States." It was a typical Cushing touch which Castro was quick to appreciate. "Ah, that is well. We are fond in Spain of appropriate historical allusions."[53]

The document of indemnity, dated February 7, 1875, was signed March 5. At long last this phase of the *Virginius* negotiations was concluded.

Finis could not be written to the affair until Spain punished the man Americans considered responsible for the executions, Juan D. Burriel, and from the moment of arrival in Spain, Cushing had urged punishment. The United States had a firmer foundation for its demand for disciplinary action against Burriel than for the indemnity. As both Fish and Cushing endlessly reminded the Spanish, the protocol between Fish and Polo had promised to punish guilty officials. "Some things," Fish told Mantilla, "are not proper subjects for arbitration." Fish was incensed by a report that Burriel had published an article in the *Revue des Deux Mondes* in which he defended his conduct. Mantilla might well have asked the secretary some embarrassing questions in return for there was no record of any legal action by the Americans against either the Robertses or their agent Patterson, all of whom had been involved in the fraud leading to the incident. Instead, Mantilla answered only that the general had been censured and his promotion denied. This, he thought, "might be regarded as punishment." On the contrary, said Fish, it was "not punishment but only refusal of reward."[54]

Cushing was not so fervent about this issue and believed that Spain had suitably recognized the illegality of the executions. At the beginning of the crisis the government had consulted leading jurists and all "were unanimously of the opinion that there was no legal justification for the proceedings. . . at Santiago de Cuba."[55] On this question the minister made plain that the United States expected Spain to punish those responsible, Burriel in particular. Castro avoided the situation as though hoping it would be forgotten or that indemnifying the survivors would satisfy his opponents.[56]

After settlement of the indemnity Cushing had assured the secretary of state he was keeping his eye on the Burriel case. The general by this time had disappeared from public view, "going it is said, to some obscure corner of Galicia." The savage warfare with the Carlists had seen many incidents similar to the Santiago executions, and popular condemnation of the Carlists for shooting prisoners was widespread. This made it impossible for anyone to come to Burriel's defense. Cushing reported that the general was denied promotion, his action condemned both by President Serrano and King Alfonso; his deeds had caused Spain to be soundly criticized, which the Spanish were used to, although this time it had cost them a great deal of money.[57]

Other forces were marshaled against the erstwhile Cuban commander. Sir Henry Layard went to the minister of state to second the demand that Burriel be brought to trial.[58] Cushing then received an answer to his notes, which after much hedging confided that action was being brought against the Santiago authorities. To the American minister's chagrin, Madrid's newspapers up to that time had carried only one item concerning Burriel, news of promotion from brigadier to major general. Writing to the Conde de Casa-Valencia, Cushing could only remark he was glad to hear that Burriel's recent promotion had not made him immune from prosecution.[59]

But it was not until April 21, 1876, that the American minister learned that the Supreme Council of War had decided to investigate the general, and that a prosecutor and secretary had been appointed for the effort. In June this group shifted responsibility to the Supreme Tribunal of the navy.[60] The slowness of Spanish justice or else delaying tactics thus saw to it that two and a half years had passed before a forum was found for the case. Nor was this all. To initiate an investigation and designate a tribunal was not tantamount to a decision, and in February, 1877, Cushing reported the trial still pending, awaiting documents from Cuba.[61]

The general nonetheless outwitted his critics, for on December 24, 1877, in his obscure corner of Galicia, he died. If some of his countrymen had abhorred his actions there were others, especially in Cuba, who had seen him as one of Spain's few vigorous soldiers, dealing justice and death to rebels and filibusters. His death notice in Havana's *Diario da la Marina* hailed the firmness of his character as shown at Santiago. The notice ended somewhat ponderously, "May the earth be light upon him."[62]

CHAPTER ELEVEN

Conclusions

IN looking back over the *Virginius* affair of 1873 one can see a significance that transcends the brief crisis in Spanish-American relations. There is the effect of the incident on the law of nations, where the positions of the United States and Spain both appear to have received reinforcement by contemporary and later experts. The Spanish failed to obtain support for their claim that the crew of the ship were pirates and thereby punishable as outlaws. That a nation whose colonies had been besieged by sea rovers since the days of Drake and Morgan might apply the term "pirate" to insurgent forces was understandable. But in this contention the Spanish government probably was wrong. A twentieth-century legal authority has written that Americans customarily have shown reluctance "to treat as piratical the operations of insurgent vessels. . . when directed solely against persons and property associated with governments to be overthrown."[1] This view has found much support. By definition piracy is an unauthorized act of violence committed by a pirate vessel on the open sea against another vessel with intent to plunder (*animo furandi*).[2] The crew of the *Virginius*, however illegal the voyage under both American and Spanish law, had shown no intention to plunder and therefore had not placed themselves beyond authority.[3] If the Spanish had reason for watching the ship, and for seizure if it entered Cuban territorial waters, they should not have considered it a pirate. Over thirty years after the passions of the *Virginius* had cooled, John Bassett Moore adjudged the men wrongfully executed.[4] A British authority agreed: "When the *Virginius* was captured she had committed no act of piracy. . . no excuse existed for regarding the vessel and crew as piratical at the moment of capture."[5]

While lawyers have accepted the American position that the *Virginius* was not a pirate, there was another legal problem, namely, whether the seizure was itself proper. There has been no support for the contemporary American charge of impropriety. By flying the American flag the *Virginius* did not protect itself from capture. Former Secretary of the Treasury George Boutwell, an able lawyer, felt strongly about this matter and in December, 1873, wrote President Grant his opinion. There could be no question, he said, that in this regard Spain was in the right. The ship "had no right to carry the flag of the United States." The flag "was not a protection to the *Virginius* within the waters of Spain." Moreover it "could not have been a protection anywhere upon the open sea."[6] Failure to halt ships because of the flags they flew would help only those individuals willing to sail under false colors. Such opinions have been ventured down to the present day; the law of nations in this regard has not changed since the time of Secretary Fish and President Grant. The Lauterpacht revision of Oppenheim's *International Law*, perhaps the leading twentieth-century authority, concludes with reference to the *Virginius:* "That a vessel sailing under another state's flag can nevertheless be seized on the high seas in case she is sailing to a port of the capturing state for the purpose of an invasion or bringing material help to insurgents there is no doubt."[7]

Ownership was the crucial issue. When the investigation in New York had proved that Spanish nationals, albeit rebellious ones, had paid for the *Virginius,* the ship became Spanish property. Two American experts have so put the issue: "Jurisdiction depends on ownership, not on certificate of registry."[8] The American Lawyer James Brown Scott has written that the *Virginius* was "rightly captured by the Spanish authorities, provided it was, and such was the fact, in the employ of Cuban insurgents."[9] Registry did not matter. After the experiences he described in *Two Years Before the Mast* Richard Henry Dana had left the sea for the courtroom to become one of the nation's leading authorities on international law, and in a Boston newspaper in January, 1874, he contended that ownership by Spanish subjects gave Spain jurisdiction over the vessel. The ship's registry notwithstanding, it was proper for nations having cause to arrest a vessel to "go behind such a document to ascertain the jurisdictional fact which gives character to the document, and not the document to the fact."[10] To quote the later judgment of J. B. Moore, "It is a fundamental principle that ships on the high seas are under the protection of the country to which they belong and are for jurisdictional purposes treated as part of its territory."[11]

There was also the issue of self-defense, justifying seizure.[12] In the judgment of a notable British legal text of the time, the Spanish had "ample reason" for seizing the ship either in Cuban waters or on the high seas because of self-defense. A nation was permitted to exercise the right of self-preservation if an attack was made on its territory, and the threat was such that "to seek out and destroy the enemy" would constitute the best means of defense. "If a state possesses the right of self-preservation, it must possess it in time of peace as well as of war," on sea as well as on land, and the right would include "defense which prevents as well as that which repels attack."[13] Years later Charles Cheney Hyde, a former solicitor of the Department of State, wrote that "On grounds of self-defense an aggrieved state may subject a foreign ship to restraint on the high seas," and that in the case of the *Virginius* there "was no duty on the Spanish authorities to refrain from seizing the vessel until she entered Cuban waters."[14]

Only in a single respect did the United States have a case against Spain, and it was an argument in international equity rather than international law. In a word, there was a case in diplomacy. It was this case that the United States eventually prosecuted, and with success. Spain might have had the best of the diplomatic argument had it not been for Burriel's firing squad. The executions threatened to enlarge the dispute into war. They led to the American ultimatum for the vessel's return, "a demand that, but for this bloody tragedy, would have had no national indignation to back it, and that could never have been rightfully enforced."[15] The *Virginius* affair was an impossible diplomatic issue for a small and weak power. At the height of the crisis Theodore D. Woolsey of Yale Law School remarked in an interview that "A weak nation must be very careful how it breaks through the fine network of what is lawful, but a strong nation will do it and take the consequences."[16]

Another interesting question about the affair concerns how the United States could have avoided war in 1873 and gone to war twenty-five years later in 1898.[17] Why did Americans stop

(131)

short of war after the deaths of fifty-three citizens at the hand of a foreign power? An obvious difference between 1873 and 1898 was the relatively careful behavior of American public opinion, or perhaps one might say that the leaders of that opinion restrained any move toward rashness. The latter-day student is struck by the fact that after the shock wore off, respectable American opinion was against intervention, despite the *New York Herald* and Cuban bondholders. Charles Sumner and Carl Schurz of the Liberal Republicans desired caution and sympathy for the Spanish republic. They were joined by the Old Guard of the GOP, Senators Oliver P. Morton and Simon Cameron, men with power in Congress, who were in no hurry to have war over the *Virginius*. The leader of the New York bar, William M. Evarts, quieted the crowd in Steinway Hall. Desire for war began to diminish as reports came of doubt concerning the registration of the *Virginius* and the citizenship of its crew.

There was a newspaper press in 1873 which a later generation would describe as yellow, and yet such newspapers lacked influence in 1873. The best example of sensationalism was the *New York Herald,* but the nation's press did not base editorials on James Gordon Bennett's newspaper which was not considered respectable. When the *Herald* called for war, other papers momentarily could produce a chorus, but with appearance of doubt of the nature of the expedition the press moderated its tone, especially when Fish was being so cautious. The *New York Times* and *New York Tribune* supported the efforts for peace, and the secretary of state later thanked the editors of both papers. If the *Herald* continued to talk loudly, it was a beast braying outside the herd.[18]

One possible explanation of why the Americans turned from war in 1873 was the race question. A war with Spain might have resulted in responsibility for Cuba's mixed population of whites and blacks. The whites appeared degenerate and backward. The blacks, slave and free, presented an unattractive picture to a nation troubled in solving its own racial problems. Fish had visited Cuba in 1856 and gained an impression of the horror of slavery, and also of the perplexities that would arise from introduction of Cubans into the American political system. Many of his correspondents years later while he was in the State Department were expressing the same view.[19]

This is not to imply that in the nineties all race tensions ended. They had not. The tragic settlement of the race question for blacks would be Jim Crow and the abandonment of whatever goals had earlier been set for black equality. But the apparent resolution of the race problem in America produced a sense of confidence that other races could be managed. It was the anti-imperialists of the turn of the century who continued, like Hamilton Fish, to ponder the dilemma of extending American sovereignty over non-whites.[20]

The fact Spain was experimenting with republicanism in 1873 also was a significant factor in keeping the peace. The same "hard money elite" who supported Fish on his Cuban policy, particularly Northeastern liberals, saw the Spanish republicans as defenders of liberalism, Castelar and Pi y Margall struggling to correct centuries of injustice. If Spain had been ruled by Isabel II, they might have regarded the matter differently; Spain was a republic in 1873 and war seemed an act of fratricide. Castelar's American admirers found it unendurable that the United States might end the republican experiment in Spain through war. These individuals wrote to Fish, to their representatives in Washington, to editors.[21]

Consider, then, the change in the situation a quarter century later when the return of monarchy again had placed Spain among the more reactionary nations of Europe. Americans in 1898 saw little difference between the Sultan of Turkey, the Czar of Russia, and the Spanish Queen Mother. All three of these rulers represented autocracy, a past which Americans were destined to overturn. No one in 1898 argued on behalf of the Spanish monarchy, in the way that Senator Sumner and Carl Schurz had defended the republic twenty-five years before.

In comparing the *Virginius* affair to the War of 1898 one must consider finally the behavior of Secretary of State Hamilton Fish. A capable man, even if historians of a later day have denied him the accolade of greatness, Fish possessed a "downright power for dealing with men."[22] Among the pygmies Grant chose for his Cabinet, Fish grandly stood out. During years when many Americans were giving in to their impulses for greed, Fish (as Allan Nevins has written) had the power to say "no" and make it stick.[23] In the flurry of excitement when

(133)

news of the *Virginius* reached Washington he was unready to commit himself or his country until he had all the facts, or as many as can ever be found in such matters. When the nation seemed to desire war with Spain he played for time; even in the initial message to Sickles following the unfounded report of the deaths of the entire crew, he was cautious. Admittedly his one lapse was dangerous. After winning his case, Fish appeared ready to pursue full vindication of national honor by demanding the American flag be flying at the time of surrender. But this moment aside he was generally a voice for restraint. Fish was a realist who never lost sight of the fact that American policy must not exceed American power, and that American power should be used only in the national interest. However much he might sympathize with the rebellion in Cuba he did not believe intervention would be advantageous. This course did not win general approval.[24] The secretary of state's belief, on legal ground, that the United States should not extend recognition of belligerency of independence, and his opposition to the Cuban party in Congress, helped prevent a break. Fish's best defense of his policy was not made in any state paper or interview with a journalist but in a private letter to his son on the day before Christmas 1873:

> I do not expect that the fugitive-from-justice editor of the *New York Sun* or the wild Irishmen who run the *New York Herald,* or the Spaniard who edits *El Cronista* will be satisfied, but I have thought of the tens of thousands of wives who might have been made widows, and of the hundreds of thousands of children who might have been made orphans, in an *unnecessary* war undertaken for a dishonest vessel. There *is* a national evil worse than war, but unless the national honor, or the national existence, require war. . . then the nation should do all that it can to avoid the terrible evil. That is what I have endeavored to do.[25]

In 1898 no such personage presided over the Department of State; John Sherman of Ohio had been an important man in his time, which by then had passed. Sherman was senile in 1898, and it is well-known that President McKinley had placed him at the head of the Cabinet because the President wished to give Mark Hanna a place in the Senate. One can only speculate on what might have happened had Hamilton Fish been in the State Department in 1898 instead of Sherman.

Would a war in 1873 have been an easy affair, with Spain as defenseless as would prove the case at the end of the century? It is intriguing to imagine what might have happened if twenty-five years before the sinking of the *Maine* a war had arisen. Perhaps it was well that the United States in 1873 did not follow the advice of the *New York Herald*. The post-Appomattox contraction of the American army had reduced that once-mighty force to twenty-five thousand men hard-pressed to garrison the Indian frontier.[26] Because of the Carlist wars in Spain and the insurrection in Cuba, the Spanish army in 1873 was a large, battle-hardened force. In 1873 the United States navy was a pathetic establishment, with antiquated ships and defective equipment, as *The Nation* was careful to point out in the midst of the *Virginius* crisis. The only ironclads the United States possessed in 1873 were virtually useless. Of the best of these ships an officer remarked with unconscious humor that he did not doubt "she could be got to Cuba in calm weather."[27] As a result of the war scare in 1873 the navy the next year assembled a force at Key West for training in case it should ever be called on for war. Robley D. Evans recalled the fiasco thirty years later: "The force assembled. . . was the best we had. . . and if it had not been so serious it would have been laughable to see our condition." Evans and other officers were "dreadfully mortified" when the government allowed foreign attachés to see the ships and report home.[28] The Spanish fleet of the 1870s was modern, and if it had been free instead of paralyzed by the revolt at Cartagena it could have given the United States navy a difficult time.

It is possible to argue that Americans were equally unprepared in 1898. The difference lay in the American navy, by then a modern, efficient fighting force.[29] The Spanish-American War was a naval war; victory was achieved in a few hours at Manila Bay and off Santiago. With destruction of its squadrons Spain could not reinforce the colonies and asked for peace.

There is one intriguing similarity between the two decades; both were marked by economic depression. Whether hard times can increase a nation's bellicosity is a moot question, but the fact remains that the United States had the opportunity to go to war in the seventies and did not, while in 1898 the nation literally leaped to arms.[30] One possible explanation is that the *Virginius* episode came at the beginning of the economic recession of the seventies and was of relatively short duration. It involved a question of national honor rather than prosperity. American trade with Cuba was important but was relatively unscathed by the guerrilla operations of the war. Divisions within the revolutionary ranks between radicals and moderates hindered military strategy. The radicals wanted to invade the island's western provinces and carry out a scorched earth policy to disrupt sugar production. The moderates refused.[31] Thus the island's economic life continued much as before.

The depression of the nineties had dragged on for nearly five years before American intervention in Cuba. By then the United States had experienced a quarter century of industrial boom and bust, prosperity and depression, which led American statesmen and industrialists to seek out foreign markets as an outlet for the excess production of the nation's factories.[32] Cuba as an independent nation rather than a colony of Spain seemed to offer more promise for American trade. Independent or Spanish, Cuba now contained more American capital investments than twenty-five years earlier, and more ruthless tactics by the guerrillas (apparently having learned the lessons of the Ten Years War) caused greater dislocation to American investments and Cuban-American trade.[33] Ironically, by the spring of 1898 the depression seemed to ease and the United States had hopes that better days were returning. There is evidence that this is the danger point in any relationship between war and economic cycles; when economic recovery is underway and optimism is building, nations are most impatient with obstacles, as was the United States with Spain in the spring of 1898.[34] And, 1898 capped thirty years of frustrating diplomacy.[35]

But the seventies witnessed no war between the United States and Spain, and American politics returned to their domestic-centered routines. If the pacific end of the dispute saw an escape from involvement in Cuba, the Spanish and Cuban rebels continued to fight. The war dragged on. The *Virginius* affair marked a halfway point in the first Cuban revolution. As though the ship's capture were a portent, the revolution began to falter. There was less trouble between Spain and the United States, as if both countries had been sobered by the brush with war. The Junta's support in the United States declined. In 1874 the rebels sought to invade the western end of the island, with no success—sugar production in that region actually increased. After the monarchy was reestablished in 1875, Spain again sent out Jovellar as captain general, with twenty-five thousand men and instructions to negotiate. Rebel morale was at low ebb. In October, Spanish soldiers captured the president of the Cuban republic, Estrada Palma, and killed the leader of the rebel assembly. In February, 1878, General Arsenio Martinez Campos managed an armistice with the guerrillas at Zanjón based on a general pardon and freedom for all rebel leaders to depart Cuba. The rebellion had failed. Some of the insurrectos, like the mulatto general Antonio Maceo, continued to fight for a few months until they recognized the inevitable. Peace came to the island, until in the 1890s rebellion blazed again, the United States entered the war, and Cuba achieved independence.[36]

After the uproar over the *Virginius* the Spanish principals went their several ways. Emilio Castelar lived till the end of the century, as Spain's most respected public figure. If he never again achieved the power he once had held as president of the republic, his pen and orations did not let Spaniards forget republicanism. When he died in 1899, hope for the Spain he had worked to create—republican, liberal, confident of its values—went with him. By chance he died during one of Spain's worst times, just after an American war had taken the remnants of the country's four-hundred-year empire. A Spanish representative at the ensuing peace conference in Paris is reported to have remarked that "Victory is complete, we have lost everything."

Admiral Polo returned to Spain in the summer of 1874, his diplomatic work less appreciated by his countrymen than was the handiwork of Burriel. Secure in knowledge that he had helped avoid war, he rejoined his family.[37] In March, 1898, his son was named as minister to Washington in succession to Dupuy de Lôme, but before the younger Polo could reach Washington the two countries were at war.

The captives of the *Virginius* had had their moment of fame, and those who survived returned to what must have seemed blissful anonymity. Some of them may again have done battle for Cuba Libre, but if they did it was without the notice that accompanied the expedition of 1873. They perhaps were more cautious, as well they should have been. Perhaps they noticed what had happened to the relatives of their comrades now dead. Several pledges had been made to support Joseph Fry's family in New Orleans, but little had happened. The indemnity must have been a godsend for his family, which had been moving from place to place as rent money gave out. Other families were not so fortunate, for generally speaking the wages of heroism were oblivion and penurious existence.[38]

The Grant administration marked the last appearance in national politics for most of the officials prominent in the *Virginius* episode. Grant's appointees were not men who could remain in national life. They were too crass, too inadequate for government service. When the administration went out of office in 1877 they disappeared. Daniel Sickles's mission proved his final piece of diplomacy. His work had been far less effective than that of Polo. Upon return he embroiled himself in new intrigues. He went back to the Democratic party and a term in the House of Representatives. But he could not live down the charge that he had plotted a war. In old age he wrote to the author of a book on Spanish-American relations complaining that

> Our vacillating and timid policy in the *Virginius* affair gave Spain the impression that we were afraid of her, resulting in her defiance of our subsequent remonstrances touching her conduct in Cuba, ending in the Spanish war of 1898. Firmness on the part of General Grant in the *Virginius* question would have settled the Cuban question then and there.[39]

He died in 1914, in near poverty, still dreaming of what might have been.

The day Fish left office in 1877 he returned to Glyncliff, at Garrison, where he enjoyed a kind of retirement. He divided his time between the estate and a townhouse in New York City. Age brought a minimum of discomfort, and save for the death of his wife in 1887 he lived happily, an observer of affairs and men, "the world forgetting, by the world forgot." On the evening of

September 6, 1893, he ate a hearty supper and slept soundly, and next morning seemed in good health. While working over his books he suddenly died. As tributes poured in the men who remembered him as the architect of the Washington Conference in 1871 and of the Geneva Tribunal recalled his efforts in behalf of peace during the *Virginius* affair. Then he too was forgotten.[40] A few years later the nation turned to the fateful war over Cuba that seemed necessary as a sign of American greatness, a conflict in which in a moment of supreme irony Fish's grandson, Sergeant Hamilton Fish of the Rough Riders, was the first American killed in action.[41] That conflict would be succeeded by wars in other parts of the world until a century and more after the *Virginius* affair, the country was giving evidence of having had enough of war.

Notes

Preface

1. Richard Harding Davis, *Soldiers of Fortune* (New York: Scribners, 1897), p. 177.

2. Harry Thurston Peck, *Twenty Years of the Republic* (New York: Dodd, Mead & Co., 1920), p. 664.

3. Allan Nevins, *Hamilton Fish, the Inner History of the Grant Administration* (New York: Dodd, Mead & Co., 1937); French E. Chadwick, *The Relations of the United States and Spain* (New York: Scribner's, 1909); Robert L. Beisner, *From the Old Diplomacy to the New, 1865-1900* (New York: Crowell, 1975), pp. 52-53 offers a good brief analysis and comparison with the *Maine* incident in 1898, as does Robert H. Ferrell, *American Diplomacy* (New York: Norton, 1975), p. 384 and Thomas A. Bailey, *The Diplomatic History of the American People* (Englewood Cliffs, N.J.: Prentice-Hall, 1975), pp. 380-81.

Chapter One

1. *New York Times, New York World, New York Herald,* March 5, 1869; Allan Nevins, *Hamilton Fish, the Inner History of the Grant Administration* (New York: Dodd, Mead & Co., 1937), pp. 106-07.

2. Allan Nevins, *Hamilton Fish,* pp. 25-55; the best short surveys of sectionalism and foreign policy in the 1850s are David M. Potter, *The Impending Crisis, 1848-1861* (New York: Harper & Row, 1976), pp. 177-98, and Lloyd C. Gardner, Walter F. LaFeber and Thomas J. McCormick, *Creation of the American Empire: U.S. Diplomatic History* (Chicago: University of Chicago Press, 1973), pp. 157-84. A monograph dealing with the South's interest in expansion is Robert E. May, *The Southern Dream of a Caribbean Empire, 1854-1861* (Baton Rouge: Louisiana State University Press, 1973).

3. Reverend Daniel Tuttle interview by A.B. Keep, 1913, in John Bassett Moore Papers, Box 225, Library of Congress.

4. Warren Frederick Ilchman, *Professional Diplomacy in the United States, 1779-1939* (Chicago: University of Chicago Press, 1961), p. 20.

5. Paul L. Ford ed., *Writings of Thomas Jefferson* (New York: G. P. Putnam & Sons, 1899), p. 278.

6. J. C. Bartlett, "British Reaction to the Cuban Insurrection of 1868-1878," *Hispanic American Historical Review* 37 (1957):296-312.

7. For the ideology and activities of Young America see Donald S.

Spencer, *Louis Kossuth and Young America: A Study of Sectionalism and Foreign Policy, 1848-1852* (Columbia: University of Missouri Press, 1977); the old article by Merle Curti, "Young America," *American Historical Review* 32 (1926):34-35, is still valuable.

8. Robert Caldwell, *The López Expeditions to Cuba, 1848-51* (Princeton: Princeton University Press, 1915); Lester D. Langley, *The Cuban Policy of the United States: A Brief History* (New York: Wiley, 1968), pp. 31-36.

9. Lester Langley, *Cuban Policy of the United States*, pp. 46-49; Philip Shriver Klein, *President James Buchanan* (University Park, Pa: Pennsylvania State University Press, 1962), pp. 234-41.

10. Spanish attitudes toward the American Civil War are described in E.J. Pratt, "Spanish Opinion of the North American Civil War," *Hispanic American Historical Review* 10 (1930):14-26; Clifford L. Egan shows Cuba's importance at the time in "Cuba, Spain and the American Civil War," *Rocky Mountain Social Science Journal* 5 (1968):58-63.

11. The best recent analysis is Franklin W. Knight, *Slave Society in Cuba During the Nineteenth Century* (Madison: University of Wisconsin Press, 1970). The view that "sugar represents Spanish absolutism; tobacco, the native liberators," is in Fernando Ortiz, *Cuban Counterpoint; Tobacco,* trans, by Harriet de Onís (New York: A. A. Knopf, 1947), p. 71. Upon his arrival in the United States in 1872 as Spain's minister, Don Polo de Bernabé wrote Madrid that "The question of slavery is the touchstone of our relations with the United States." Polo de Bernabé to Foreign Minister of Spain, Nov. 15 and Oct. 29, 1872, Correspondencia, E.E. Unidos, Legajos 1473 (1870-72), Archivo del Ministerio de Asuntos Experiores, Madrid.

12. Sugar dominated Cuba's foreign trade. During the reign of Isabel II (1833-1868) the number of sugar estates doubled. Roland T. Ely, "The Old Cuba Trade; Highlights and Case Studies of Cuban-American Interdependence during the Nineteenth Century," *Business History Review* 37 (Winter, 1964):456. Restrictions on black seamen entering Cuba led to an American protest against this "inconvenience" on American commerce. Seward to John Hale, Aug. 19, 1868, Diplomatic Instructions of the Department of State, 1801-1906, Spain, National Archives.

13. Quoted in Albert Gardner Robinson, *Cuba and the Intervention* (New York: Longmans, Green and Co., 1905), p. 15.

14. Philip S. Foner, *A History of Cuba and Its Relations With the United States, 1845-1895,* 2 vols. (New York: International Pub., 1962-63) 2:164.

15. Arthur F. Corwin, *Spain and the Abolition of Slavery in Cuba,*

1817-1886 (Austin: University of Texas Press, 1967), p. 195; Foner, *A History of Cuba,* 2:125.

16. Langley, *Cuban Policy of the United States,* p. 56.

17. A short biography by a noted Cuban historian is Hermino Portell Vilá, *Céspedes: El Padre de la Patria Cubana* (Madrid: Espasa Calpe, 1931), pp. 72-86 for the beginning of the revolution; also see Elias Entralgo, *La Insurreccion de los Diez Años* (Habana, 1950).

18. C.H. Bithorn to Seward, Oct. 17, 1869, cited in Hermino Portell Vilá, *Historia de Cuba en Sus Relaciones con los Estados Unidos y España, 1853-1878,* 2 vols. (Habana: J. Montero, 1939), 2:207.

19. A defense of the Volunteers by one of their officers is Justo Zaragoza, *Las Insurrecciones en Cuba, Apuntes Para la Historia Politica de Esta Isla en Presente Siglo* (Madrid: M.G. Hernandez, 1872-73); a contemporary American account which is not unfriendly is in W.J. Sparks, "Cuba and the Cuban Insurrection," *Scribner's Monthly* 6 (May, 1873): 14-16.

20. Ramiro Guerra y Sanchez, *Guerra de los Diez Años, 1868-78,* (Habana: Cultural, 1950), 1:230-31.

21. The Cuban Junta in New York published a generally reliable account of atrocities in *The Book of Blood,* trans by Nestor Ponce de Leon y Languardia (New York: M.M. Zarzamendi, 1873).

22. Vilá, *Céspedes,* p. 106.

23. Francisco Ponte Dominguez, *Historia de la Guerra de los Diez Años,* (Habana, 1950) 2:27-28.

24. The story of a Spanish patrol can be found in "A State of Siege in Cuba," *All the Year Round* (May 27, 1871), pp. 611-12; Foner, *A History of Cuba* 2:184-89, has a good account of guerrilla war.

25. Henry C. Hall to Fish, April 1, 10, 17, 1869, Dispatches from United States Consuls in Havana, 1783-1906, National Archives.

26. A.E. Phillips to Fish, July 10, 1869, Dispatches from United States Consuls in Santiago, 1799-1900, National Archives; C.H. Bithorn (U.S. Consul at Manzanillo) to Fish, Feb. 25, 1870, Dispatches/Santiago.

27. A.E. Phillips to Fish, Aug. 29, 1869, Dispatches/Santiago.

28. DeMartz to Fish, Nov. 24, 1869, Dispatches/Santiago.

29. Foner, *A History of Cuba* 2:178, 205.

30. Phillips to Fish, April 24, July 10, Oct. 6, 1869, Dispatches/Santiago; Bithorn to Fish, Aug. 28, 1869, Dispatches/Santiago.

31. James H. Wilson, *The Life of John A. Rawlins* (New York: Neale Pub. Co., 1916), pp. 359-60.

32. Nevins, *Hamilton Fish,* p. 184.

33. Philip Wayne Powell, *Tree of Hate: Propaganda and Prejudices Affecting United States Relations With the Hispanic World* (New

(143)

York: Basic Books, 1971), pp. 117-27; see also Charles Gibson, ed., *The Black Legend: Anti-Spanish Attitudes in the Old World and the New* (New York: A.A. Knopf, 1971).

34. The British Foreign Secretary Lord Clarendon believed the Spanish were "ready to recognize the independence of the colony they now know they cannot keep," but wanted Great Britain and the United States to give them time. Clarendon to Prime Minister William Gladstone, Sept. 18, 1868, Gladstone Papers, 44134, British Museum.

35. Nevins, *Hamilton Fish,* pp. 247-48.

36. Fred Harvey Harrington, *Fighting Politician, Major General N.P. Banks* (Philadelphia: University of Pennsylvania Press, 1948), pp. 186-87.

37. Nevins, *Hamilton Fish,* p. 244.

38. Certainly the Spanish minister to Washington from 1872-74, Polo de Barnabé, looked on Fish as a friend and man of uncensurable character, "but he must mold himself to the opinion of the country, and he has the merit that on doing it he knows how to keep on middle ground." Polo de Bernabé to Foreign Minister of Spain, Dec. 6, 1872, Correspondencia, E.E. Unidos; Foner, *A History of Cuba,* 2:201-03.

39. James. B. Chapin, "Hamilton Fish and American Expansion" (Ph.D. diss., Cornell University, 1971), p. 293.

40. Ibid., p. 294.

41. Ibid., pp. 175-76.

42. Lord Clarendon to Sir Henry Layard, March 15, 1870, Lord Clarendon Private Papers, F.O. 361, Public Record Office, London; the Spanish were not above reminding Washington of the *Alabama* in difficult moments, Ministerio de Estado to López Roberts, Sept. 18, 1869, Correspondencia E.E. Unidos, Legajos 1472 (1865-69); Jerónimo Bécker, *Historia de Las Relaciones Exteriores de España Durante el Sigle XIX,* 1868-1900, (Madrid: J. Rates 1926), 3:35; Guerra y Sanchez, *Guerra de los Diez Años,* 1:356-59; James Morton Callahan, *Cuba and International Relations* (Baltimore: Johns Hopkins University Press, 1899), p. 381.

43. Arguments Fish repeated again and again. See, for instance, in entry of Oct. 3, 1873, Diary of Hamilton Fish, Fish Papers, Library of Congress.

44. *Foreign Relations of the United States, 1874* (Washington, D.C.: U.S. Government Printing Office, 1874), pp. 1001-02.

Chapter Two

1. Fish to Senator T.O. Howe, June 27, 1871, Hamilton Fish Papers, Library of Congress; Fish told Grant sarcastically that he always advised applicants for the consulate in Santiago to "take their

coffin with them, in case of appointment." Fish to Grant, Sept. 23, 1870, Fish Papers.

2. Nevins, *Hamilton Fish,* p. 190; W.A. Swanberg, *Sickles the Incredible* (New York: Scribner's, 1956), p. 306; Fish first learned to distrust Sickles when as a young lawyer the future minister passed him a bad check.

3. Klein, *President James Buchanan,* pp. 236-40.

4. Swanberg, *Sickles the Incredible,* pp. 306, 308.

5. Ibid., p. 306. Sickles was careful to remember Fish in his expenditures, sending him casks of fine sherry from Jerez. Sickles to Fish, Jan. 18, 1873, Fish Papers.

6. Adee to Young, April 9, 1873, John Russell Young Papers, Library of Congress.

7. Tyler Dennett, *John Hay: From Poetry to Politics* (New York: Dodd, Mead & Co., 1933), p.199.

8. Swanberg, *Sickles the Incredible,* pp. 344-45.

9. Ibid., pp. 333-40.

10. Ibid., p. 341; Adee to Fish, May 25, 1873, Dispatches from United States Ministers to Spain, 1792-1906, National Archives.

11. Swanberg, *Sickles the Incredible,* p. 341.

12. Interview with Polo de Bernabé, entry of April 17, 1873, Fish diary.

13. Quoted in J.B. Trend, *The Origin of Modern Spain* (New York: Russell & Russell, 1965), p. 24.

14. Edward Henry Strobel, *The Spanish Revolution, 1868-75* (Boston: Small, Maynard & Co., 1898), p. 179; Raymond Carr, *Spain, 1808-1939* (Oxford: Oxford University Press, 1966), p. 330.

15. Trend, *The Origins of Modern Spain,* pp. 26-27. The most thorough study is C.A.M. Hennessy, *Pi y Margall and the Federal Republican Movement, 1868-74* (Oxford: Oxford University Press, 1962). One need not accept Raymond Carr's statement, "The collapse of army discipline was inevitable when a party committed to the abolition of conscription came to power," to appreciate his analysis; Carr, *Spain, 1808-1939,* p. 331.

16. Strobel, *The Spanish Revolution,* p. 223; A.A. Adee, "A Prefatory Note on Spanish Politics," *The Century Magazine,* 35 (November, 1898): 141. Army discipline had degenerated to the point where President Nicholas Salmeron could say to a general, "If you can get one soldier to fire his rifle at a Catonalist, you have saved order;" Carr, *Spain, 1808-1939,* p. 344.

17. Alvey A. Adee, "Reminiscences of Castelar," *The Century Magazine* (March, 1886): 792-94: For Castelar in power see Alvaro Figueroa y Torres Romanones, *Los Cuarto Presidentes de la Primera*

(145)

Republic Española (Espasa-Calpa, S.A., 1939), pp. 126-47; David Hannay, *Don Emilio Castelar* (London, 1898); Don Manuel Gonzales Araco, *Castelar, Su Vida y Su Muerte* (Madrid: Establecimiento Tip "Sucesores de Rivadenegra," 1900).

Chapter Three

1. Carlos Manuel de Céspedes y Quesada, *Manuel de Quesada y Loynez* (Habana: Imprinta "El Siglo XX," 1925), p. 105. Ramiro Guerra y Sánchez, *Historia de la Nacion Cubana,* 10 vols. (Habana: Editorial Historia de la Nación Cubana, 1952), 5:28.

2. Deposition of Adolfo de Varone in *Foreign Relations, 1874,* p. 1048.

3. Ibid., pp. 1001-02; *New York Times,* Dec. 31, 1873.

4. *Foreign Relations, 1874,* pp. 1002-03, 1009.

5. Deposition of Francis E. Shepperd, *Foreign Relations, 1874,* p. 1009.

6. "The *Virginius* Case," *The American Law Review,* 8 (April, 1874): 474.

7. Deposition of Edward Greenwood, *Foreign Relations, 1874,* p. 1029; affidavit of Thomas Gallagher, ibid., p. 1036.

8. Ibid., p. 1030; see also Carlos Céspedes y Quesada, *Manuel de Quesada y Loynaz,* pp. 107-24.

9. Shepperd and Greenwood Depositions, *Foreign Relations,* 1874, pp. 1012, 1030-31.

10. Deposition of Francis Bower, ibid., pp. 1018-19.

11. Deposition of Charles Smith, ibid., p. 1022.

12. Shepperd Deposition, ibid., pp. 1009-10.

13. Smith Deposition, ibid., p. 1027.

14. The Navy had begun to build up in the Caribbean in response to the Cuban situation and commanders were under orders to stop any attempt by the Spanish to capture American vessels unless they were landing troops. Fish had already mentioned the *Virginius* to Secretary of the Navy Robeson in connection with civil war in Venezuela. Cited in John Bassett Moore, *A Digest of International Law,* 8 vols. (Washington: U.S. Government Printing Office, 1906) 2:901-02. *New York Times,* July 16 and Nov. 12, 1873. Richard W. Turk, "Strategy and Foreign Policy: The United States Navy in the Caribbean, 1865-1913," (Ph.D diss, Fletcher School of Law and Diplomacy, 1968), p. 86.

15. Seaton Schroeder, *A Half Century of Naval Service* (New York: D. Appleton & Co., 1922), p. 67.

16. "The *Virginius* Case," p. 481.

17. Schroeder, *A Half Century of Naval Service,* p. 68.

18. Ibid.

19. Ibid.; *New York Times,* July 17, 1873, reported that Reed later said he would notify Washington that the *Virginius* should have its register taken away. Reed said the Spanish would be justified in sinking the ship on the high seas to Cuba, but in a neutral port he could do nothing but extend protection to it.

20. Pearne to Davis, July 17, 1873, Dispatches from the United States Consuls in Kingston, Jamaica, 1796-1906, National Archives. In fact the *Bazan* came into Kingston harbor after the *Virginius* but made no more threatening moves. See *British and Foreign State Papers, 1973-74,* 65 (London, 1881).

21. *British and Foreign State Papers, 1873-74,* pp. 132-33.

22. Ibid., p. 133.

23. Affidavit of Evaristo Sanchez Sunsunegeri, Department of Justice, Source Chronological Files, Record Group 60, National Archives.

24. *New York Times,* Nov. 8, 1873; Emeterio S. Santovenia y Echaide, *Huellas de Gloria* (Habana, 1944), p. 121.

25. *New York Times,* Nov. 8.

26. Ibid.; Francisco Calcagno, *Diccionario Biografica Cubana* (New York: N. Ponce de Leon, 1878), p. 664.

27. J.S. Grant and John Fiske, eds., *Appleton's Encyclopedia of American Biography* 36 (New York: D. Appleton & Co., 1888). Ryan's early years are clouded in mystery. His place and year of birth have also been listed as 1843 in Toronto.

28. Jeanie Mort Walker, *Life of Captain Joseph Fry the Cuban Martyr* (Hartford: J.B. Burr Pub. Co., 1875) is a biography written after his death in an effort to secure financial help for his family. Although it must be used with caution, the author had access to many of Fry's letters, no longer extant. For the most recent account of Fry see Jim Dan Hill, "Captain Joseph Fry of S.S. Virginius", *The American Neptune,* 36 (April, 1976): 88-100.

29. Captain Edwin L. Brady to Fish, Nov. 15, 1873, Miscellaneous Letters of the Department of State, Nov. 1-17, 1873, National Archives.

30. William Baynard to Burt Capron, Nov. 7, 1873, James A. Garfield to Fish, Dec. 16, 1873, Miscellaneous Letters of the Department of State, Dec. 1-18, 1873.

31. Testimony of Henry King, Correspondence Relating to the Seizure of the *Virginius,* National Archives.

32. Testmony of George Burke, ibid.

33. Petition from Citizens of Salem, New Jersey to Hamilton Fish,

Nov. 12, 1873, Miscellaneous Letters.

34. *New York Times,* Nov. 16, 1873.

35. Ibid.

36. Ibid.

37. Sunsunegeri Affidavit; Spencer St. John British consul in Port-au-Prince, to Lord Granville, Nov. 8, 1873, F.O. 72/1637, Public Office, London.

38. Sunsunegeri Affidavit.

39. Ibid.

40. Spencer St. John to Lord Granville, Nov. 8, 1973, F.O. 72/1637, PRO London.

41. Sunsunegeri Affidavit.

Chapter Four

1. Report of Captain Dionisio Costilla printed in *El Eco de Cuba,* Nov. 15, 1873, enclosure, Dispatches/Havana, Dispatches Relating to the Capture of the *Virginius.*

2. *Foreign Relations, 1874,* p. 1077.

3. Costilla's Report.

4. Ibid; *Foreign Relations, 1874,* p. 1077.

5. Rudolph de Cordova, "The *Virginius* Incident and Cuba," *Nineteenth Century* 60 (Dec., 1906): 979.

6. Sunsunegeri Affidavit.

7. de Cordova, "*Virginius* Incident and Cuba," p. 979.

8. Ibid.

9. Sunsunegeri Affidavit.

10. Walker, *Life of Joseph Fry,* pp. 241-46.

11. Ibid.

12. Costilla's Report.

13. de Cordova, "*Virginius* Incident and Cuba," p. 980.

14. *Foreign Relations, 1874,* p. 1077.

15. Walker, *Life of Joseph Fry,* pp. 257-58; *New York Times,* Dec. 6, 1873.

16. Walker, *Life of Joseph Fry,* pp. 257-58.

17. Schmitt received no criticism for what took place at Santiago. Henry Hall, his superior at Havana, credited him with doing all that could be done. Hall to Schmitt, Nov. 15, 1873, General Correspondence, Havana Consulate, National Archives.

18. Samuel Flagg Bemis, *Pinckney's Treaty,* rev. ed. (New Haven: Yale University Press, 1960), pp. 348-49.

19. *Foreign Relations, 1874,* p. 1074.

20. *Foreign Relations, 1874,* p. 1060.

21. Ibid., p. 1059.

22. Ibid., p. 1064.

23. Schmitt to Hall, Nov. 3, 1873, Dispatches/Havana.

24. *Foreign Relations*, 1874, p. 1065.

25. Schmitt to Hall, Nov. 6, 1873, Dispatches/Havana; Brooks to John V. Crawford, Acting Consul General Havana, Nov. 8, *British and Foreign State Papers*, 1873-74, 65, pp. 137-38.

26. Schmitt to Hall, Nov. 3, Dispatches/Havana.

27. *New York Times*, Dec. 5, 1873. The account of the execution is based on the description of Francis Coffin, second mate of the *Morning Star*. Coffin's account matches that of other observers and he gives the lie to the many sensational stories that circulated of the executions.

28. Rudolph de Cordova, "*Virginius* Incident and Cuba," p. 980.

29. *New York Times*, Dec. 6, 1873.

30. *Harper's Weekly*, 17 (Dec. 6, 1873).

31. *New York Times*, Dec. 6.

32. Walker, *Life of Joseph Fry*, p. 254.

33. *British and Foreign State Papers*, 1873-74, pp. 136-37.

34. Ibid., p. 138.

35. Ibid.

36. Ibid.

37. de Cordova, "*Virginius* Incident and Cuba," p. 982.

38. Ibid., p. 982-83.

39. *British and Foreign State Papers*, 1873-74, p. 146.

40. Ship's Log, H.M.S. *Niobe*, Nov. 3, 1873-July 23, 1874, Adm. 53/1027, Public Record Office, London.

41. *British and Foreign State Papers*, 1873-74, p. 138.

42. *British and Foreign State Papers*, 1873-74, p. 138.

43. Ibid.

44. John V. Crawford, Acting Consul General, Havana, to Lord Granville, Nov. 20, 1873, F.O. 72/1638, Public Record Office, London.

45. Walker, *Life of Joseph Fry*, p. 454.

46. Ibid., p. 452.

47. Ibid., p. 453.

48. de Cordova, "*Virginius* Incident and Cuba," p. 454.

49. Walker, *Life of Joseph Fry*, p. 454.

50. *New York Times*, Dec. 5, 1873.

51. *Foreign Relations, 1874*, pp. 1073-74.

52. Ibid., pp. 1074-75.

53. Ibid., p. 1075.

54. Ibid.

55. Ibid., p. 1076.

56. de Cordova, "*Virginius* Incident and Cuba," p. 984.

57. *British and Foreign State Papers, 1873-74*, p. 139. The last

group of men executed did not contain any American citizens or British subjects.

58. *Niobe* Log, Nov. 3, 1873-July 23, 1874.

59. *British and Foreign State Papers, 1873-74,* p. 139.

Chapter Five

1. *National Republican,* Nov. 4, 1873.

2. Hall to Fish, Dec. 5, 1873, *Foreign Relations, 1874,* p. 1052.

3. Fish is open to censure for making no effort to send a gunboat to Santiago as soon as he heard of capture, for he was aware of the summary justice dealt to prisoners, Vilá, *Historia de Cuba, 1853-1878,* 2:431-32. It was too late to save Ryan but possible that a vessel from the navy base at Key West could have reached Santiago in time to save Fry and the crew.

4. Sickles to Fish, Nov. 7, *Foreign Relations, 1874,* p. 922.

5. Fish diary, Nov. 7.

6. Nevins, *Hamilton Fish,* p. 667. The memoranda are among Fish's papers.

7. Fish diary, Nov. 7.

8. Fish diary, Nov. 8.

9. Fish regarded Thornton highly, but the Englishman viewed the American with restraint. Fish, Thornton wrote, "has no exalted idea of the entire credit which one ought to be able to give to the word of a gentleman," but was "perhaps better than most Americans and is not unpleasant to deal with." Thornton to Clarendon, June 14, 1870, Clarendon Papers, F.O. 361, Public Record Office, London.

10. Thornton had already heard that the ship's right to fly the American flag was "doubtful." Thornton to Granville, Nov. 10, 1873, F.O. 72/1637.

11. Ibid.

12. Fish diary, Nov. 8.

13. Fish diary, Nov. 11.

14. Ibid.

15. Ibid.

16. Fish diary, Nov. 12.

17. *Foreign Relations, 1874,* p. 927.

18. The Spanish historian Bécker points out Captain General Jovellar did not know consuls could enter claims for damages in their districts. He thought that only diplomatic agents could do that. Bécker, *Relaciones Exteriores de Espana,* 3:165-66.

19. Fish diary, Nov. 13, 1873. Thornton told Fish it would be impossible for the Spanish government to accept. Fish agreed, adding

Spain had not yet convinced itself "that the Netherlands and the Spanish American Republics were independent nations," Thornton to Granville, Nov. 17, F.O. 72/1637. In the Archivo del Ministerio de Asuntos Exteriores, Madrid, there is no copy of what must have been a very interesting dispatch from Polo.

20. Fish diary, Nov. 13.

21. Fish diary, Nov. 14.

22. Ibid.

23. Ibid.

24. Hall to Fish, Nov. 15, *Foreign Relations, 1874*, p. 1071; Fish diary, Nov. 14.

25. Fish to Sickles, Nov. 15, *Foreign Relations, 1874*, p. 938.

26. Fish diary, Nov. 15.

27. Ibid.

28. Indeed the secretary seemed to take the attitude that the men aboard the *Virginius* were asking for their fate. In an interview he was reported as saying of the death of Santa Rosa: "He has given me a great deal of trouble," referring to an earlier incident when the State Department had saved him from captivity because of American citizenship. The Cuban was "foolhardy" to try again. *Chicago Daily Tribune*, Nov. 11; *New Orleans Daily Picayune*, Nov. 11.

29. Frank Luther Mott, *American Journalism, A History, 1690-1960* (New York: MacMillan, 1964), p. 406. See also Frederick Hudson, *Journalism in the United States, From 1690 to 1872* (New York: Harper & Brothers, 1873).

30. "Washington News," *Harpers*, 48 (Jan., 1874): 225-36.

31. Mott, *American Journalism, A History*, p. 406.

32. *National Republican*, Nov. 12.

33. *New York Times*, Nov. 6.

34. Ibid., Nov. 9.

35. *New York Post*, Nov. 13.

36. *New York Times*, Nov. 13.

37. *New York Tribune*, Nov. 10.

38. *New York Herald*, Nov. 10.

39. Ibid., Nov. 13.

40. *New Orleans Daily Picayune*, Nov. 22; Walker, *Life of Joseph Fry*, pp. 297-98.

41. Walker, *Life of Joseph Fry*, pp. 293-94; *New Orleans Daily Picayune*, Nov. 14.

42. Thornton to Granville, Nov. 16, F.O. 72/1637.

43. *New Orleans Daily Picayune*, Nov. 20; *Atlanta Constitution*, Nov. 22.

44. *New Orleans Daily Picayune*, Nov. 23.

45. *New York Times,* Nov. 13.

46. Interviews with Cox, Evarts, and Pierrepont in *New York Times,* Nov. 15.

47. Pierrepont to Fish, Nov. 13, Fish Papers.

48. J. C. Bancroft Davis to Fish, Nov. 13, 1873, Fish Papers.

49. Pierrepont to Fish, Nov. 13, Fish Papers.

50. Pierrepont to Fish, Nov. 14, Fish Papers.

51. Pierrepont to Fish, Nov. 17, Fish Papers.

52. *New York Times,* Nov. 13.

53. *New York Tribune,* Nov. 14.

54. *New York Times,* Nov. 15; (see also the articles on the naval buildup in) *New York Times,* Nov. 13.

55. "How Should We Fight Spain?" *The Nation,* 17 (Dec. 4, 1873): 364.

56. *New York Times,* Nov. 15.

57. *National Republican,* Nov. 17.

58. Microfilm Series 1, Subseries B. General Correspondence, Grant Papers, Library of Congress.

59. Nevins, *Hamilton Fish,* p. 668.

60. Thornton to Granville, Nov. 18, cited in Christopher J. Bartlett, "British Reaction to the Cuban Insurrection," p. 306.

61. J. C. Bancroft Davis to Fish, Nov. 9, Fish Papers.

62. *New York Times,* Nov. 18.

63. Ibid; Brainerd Dyer, *The Public Career of William M. Evarts* (Berkeley: University of California Press, 1933), p. 161.

64. *New York Times,* Nov. 18.

65. Ibid.

66. For Sumner's actions on Cuba see David Donald, *Charles Sumner and the Rights of Man* (New York: A.A. Knopf, 1970), pp. 417-19.

67. *New York Tribune,* Nov. 18, 1873. Sumner's correspondence shows much support for his views, Sumner Papers, Widener Library, Harvard University.

68. "The Reasons for Keeping Cool About It," *The Nation,* 17 (Nov. 20, 1873): 332-34.

69. *Savannah News,* Nov. 22, 1873; *Richmond Whig,* Nov. 15.

70. *Atlanta Constitution,* Nov. 22; *New Orleans Daily Picayune,* Nov. 22. An interesting study of one city's reaction is Henry A. Kmen, "Remember the *Virginius:* New Orleans and Cuba in 1873," *Louisiana History,* 11 (1970): 313-31.

71. *New York Herald,* Nov. 23; *The Christian Union,* Nov. 19.

Chapter Six

1. Sickles to Fish, Oct. 31, 1873, Dispatches/Spain.

2. *The Nation,* 17 (Dec. 11, 1873): 378.

3. Sickles to Fish, Nov. 2, Dispatches/Spain.

4. Ibid. Sickles did not confine his bias to his dispatches. He told the British minister, Sir Henry Layard, that Castelar was no "better than the others," and read his dispatches to Washington to most of the diplomatic corps in Madrid; Nov. 7, 1873, Layard Papers, vol. 195, British Museum, London.

5. Captain General D. Joaquin Jovellar's telegram announcing the capture is in Ildefonso Antonio Bermejo, *Historia de la Interinidad y Guerra Civil de España desde 1868,* (Madrid: R. Labajos, 1877), 3: 561. According to Jovellar the capture took place "una legua," three and a half miles, from Jamaica; Sickles to Fish, Nov. 7, *Foreign Relations, 1874,* p. 923.

6. Sickles to Fish, Nov. 7, *Foreign Relations, 1874,* p. 923. Sickles learned the next day that some liberal members of the Cortes had asked Castelar to intercede on behalf of the prisoners.

7. Sickles to Fish, Nov. 8, *Foreign Relations, 1874,* pp. 924-25.

8. Ibid., p. 926.

9. Sickles to Fish, Nov. 12, *Foreign Relations, 1874,* p. 931. Castelar perhaps did not know that Jovellar was arguing it was necessary to have more executions; Bermejo, *Guerra Civil de España,* 3:562-63.

10. Sickles to Fish, Nov. 13, *Foreign Relations, 1874,* p. 932.

11. Ibid., p. 932-33.

12. Ibid., p. 933. The British minister had suspicions at first that Castelar had not sent orders to Cuba to delay the executions and was only deceiving Sickles when he said he had; Layard to Granville, Nov. 16, Layard Papers, vol. 195. According to Jerónimo Bécker, downed cable lines between Havana and Santiago caused Castelar's orders to reach Santiago three days after the last executions, Bécker, *Relaciones Exteriores,* 3:167.

13. Sickles to Fish, Nov. 13, *Foreign Relations, 1874,* p. 933.

14. Ibid., p. 934.

15. Ibid.

16. Ibid., p. 935. By now the Spanish government had received Polo's cable warning of the gravest complications; Polo to Carvajal, Nov. 13, cited in Jerónimo Bécker, *Relaciones Exteriores,* 3:168.

17. Sickles to Carvajal, Nov. 14, 1873, *Foreign Relations, 1874,* p. 937.

18. Fish to Sickles, Nov. 14, *Foreign Relations, 1874,* p. 936.

19. Fish to Sickles, Nov. 15, *Foreign Relations, 1874,* p. 938.

20. Layard reported to Granville that the Madrid press was unanimous in urging the government to resist any interference by the United States and in approving the shootings, Nov. 14, Layard Papers, vol.

194; Sickles to Fish, Nov. 16, *Foreign Relations, 1874,* p. 940.

21. So the British minister believed; Layard to Granville, Nov. 19, F.O. 72/1637.

22. Sickles's language was characterized by the British minister as "such as is rarely found in diplomatic correspondence, but it was perhaps not altogether unjustified," Layard to Granville, confidential, Nov. 19, F.O. 72/1637. Sickles to Carvajal, Nov. 15, *Foreign Relations, 1874,* pp. 941-42.

23. Granville to Layard, Nov. 15, *British and Foreign State Papers, 1873-74,* pp. 99-100.

24. Unpublished Memoirs, Layard Papers, III, British Museum, London.

25. Cabinet Minutes, Nov. 15, Cab. 41/5/38, Public Record Office, London.

26. Gordon Waterfield, *Layard of Nineveh* (New York:Praeger, 1968), p. 321.

27. Ibid., p. 329.

28. *London Times,* Nov. 10.

29. Layard to Granville, Nov. 18, *British and Foreign State Papers, 1873-74,* pp. 105-07.

30. Layard Memoirs, III, p. 61.

31. Layard to Granville, Nov. 18, F.O. 72/1637.

32. Layard to Granville, private, Nov. 16, Layard Papers, vol. 194.

33. Layard to Granville, Nov. 17, F.O. 72/1637.

34. Cabinet Minutes, Nov. 17, Cab. 41/5/39, Public Record Office.

35. Layard to Granville, Nov. 16, Layard Papers, vol. 194; Layard to Granville, Nov. 18, Layard Papers, vol. 195.

36. Granville to Layard, Nov. 17, *British and Foreign State Papers, 1873-74,* p. 103.

37. Christopher J. Bartlett, "British Reaction to the Cuban Insurrection of 1868-1878," *Hispanic American Historical Review,* 37 (1957): 299-300, 309. Cabinet Minutes, Nov. 17, 1873, Cab. 41/5/39, Public Record Office. Layard to Granville, Nov. 18, 1873, Layard Papers, vol. 195.

38. Layard to Granville, Nov. 18, Layard Papers, vol 195.

39. Layard to Granville, private, Nov. 18, Layard Papers, Correspondence Register.

40. Ibid. Layard suspected at least one article in the radical journal *El Imparcial,* to be the work of Carvajal; *El Imparcial,* Nov. 16. The semi-official *Diario Español,* Nov. 16, called for giving Sickles his passport; *El Imparcial,* Nov. 14, called on all Spaniards to rise above their parties to defend Spanish honor from Yankee intervention.

41. Layard to Granville, Nov. 18, Layard Papers, vol. 195.

42. Layard to Granville, private, Nov. 19, Layard Papers, Correspondence Register; Sickles to Fish, Nov. 21, *Foreign Relations, 1874,* p. 957.

43. Layard to Granville, Nov. 18, F.O. 72/1637.

44. Carvajal to Sickles, Nov. 18, *Foreign Relations, 1874,* p. 950.

45. Layard to Granville, private, Nov. 19, 1873, F. O. 72/1637.

46. Layard to Granville, confidential, Nov. 19, F.O. 72/1637.

47. Layard Memoirs, III, p. 57.

48. Layard to Granville, confidential, Nov. 19, F.O. 72/1637.

49. Layard Memoirs, III, p. 327.

50. Sickles to Fish, Nov. 19, *Foreign Relations, 1874,* p. 954.

Chapter Seven

1. *New York Times,* Nov. 23, 1873.

2. Bancroft to Fish, Dec. 8, Dispatches from United States Ministers to the German States and Germany, 1799-1906, National Archives.

3. *New York Times,* Dec. 7.

4. Thornton to Granville, Nov. 19, F.O. 72/1637.

5. Fish diary, Nov. 20.

6. Hall to Fish, Cable, Nov. 18, *Foreign Relations, 1874,* pp. 1077-78.

7. Fish diary, Nov. 18.

8. Fish diary, Nov. 18; Edwin L. Brady to Fish, Nov. 15, Fish Papers; Fish to Sickles, Nov. 19, *Foreign Relations, 1874,* p. 955.

9. Layard to Granville, private, Nov. 22, Layard Papers, vol. 195. Layard believed the Spanish had tried to intimidate Sickles by their newspaper attacks which "only made matters worse and strengthened his hands."

10. Layard Memoirs, III, p. 63.

11. Ibid.; Thornton to Granville, Nov. 21, F.O. 72/1637.

12. Layard to Granville, Nov. 19, Layard Papers, vol. 195.

13. Waterfield, *Layard of Nineveh,* pp. 337-39.

14. Layard to Granville, Nov. 20, F.O. 72/1637; Layard Memoirs, III, p. 63.

15. Sickles to Fish, Nov. 20, *Foreign Relations, 1874,* p. 956.

16. Ibid.

17. Fish diary, Nov. 21.

18. Ibid.

19. Fish to Sickles, Nov. 21, *Foreign Relations, 1874,* p.957.

20. James Ford Rhodes in his *History of the United States, 1859-1877* (New York: MacMillan, 1906) makes the charge that Sickles sent Spain's harshest expressions to Washington by cable, while send-

ing the Madrid Cabinet's more conciliatory statements by way of the regular mails, pp. 29-36. This is misleading for Sickles was dealing with Carvajal, while Castelar was presenting the real plans of the government after November 20 directly to Fish through Polo.

21. Sickles to Moran, Nov. 19, 1873, quoted in Benjamin Moran's Journal, Nov. 24, Moran Papers, Library of Congress. "Yes, " Moran had mused to himself, "the old time does come back even to me as to Sickles, the stiff days of Buchanan when this was called the fighting legation."

22. Sickles to Fish, Nov. 26, *Foreign Relations, 1874,* p. 960.

23. Sickles to Fish, Nov. 26, ibid., p. 961.

24. Montaigne to Washburne, n. d., Elihu Washburne Papers, vol. 83, Library of Congress. Montaigne went to see Fish and afterward wrote Washburne, "Excuse me for speaking disrespectfully of my 'superior,' but I didn't like him at all. Governor Fish did not ask me to sit down, said he was much engaged and I therefore got as cool as I could out of 'the presence'."

25. Fish diary, Nov. 27; memorandum, Nov. 27, *Foreign Relations, 1874,* p. 986.

26. Memorandum, Nov. 27, *Foreign Relations, 1874,* pp. 986-87.

27. Fish diary, Nov. 27.

28. William B. Hesseltine, *Ulysses S. Grant, Politician* (New York: Dodd, Mead & Co., 1935), p. 303.

29. Memorandum, Nov. 27, *Foreign Relations, 1874,* pp. 986-87.

30. Fish to Sickles, Nov. 28, *Foreign Relations, 1874,* p. 966.

31. Swanberg, *Sickles the Incredible,* p. 348; Sickles to Fish, Nov. 28, *Foreign Relations, 1874,* pp. 966-67.

32. Bécker, *Relaciones Exteriores de España,* 3:176-78; *Foreign Relations, 1874,* pp. 987-88.

33. Polo to Fish, Dec. 1, *Foreign Relations, 1874,* p. 988.

34. Fish to Polo, Dec. 2, ibid., *Foreign Relations, 1874,* p.989.

35. Fish diary, Dec. 3; Sickles to Fish, Dec. 3, *Foreign Relations, 1874,* p. 972.

Chapter Eight

1. Fish diary, Dec. 4, 1873.

2. Ibid., Dec.5.

3. Ibid.

4. Fish diary, Dec. 6.

5. Ibid., Dec. 7.

6. Ibid.

7. Ibid.

8. Fish diary, Dec. 8.

(156)

9. Ibid., Dec. 9.

10. Letterbook 6D of J.C.B. Davis, Dec. 9, J. Bancroft Davis Papers, Library of Congress.

11. Like Captain Fry, Sheppherd was a U.S. Naval Academy graduate who entered Confederate service and then could not find employment following the war. *Foreign Relations, 1874,* pp. 1009-12.

12. Ibid., pp. 1013-14. Bliss, in a letter to Fish, denounced Bowen as a former slaver and participant in the "coolie trade;" Fish Papers, Nov. 25, 1873.

13. *Foreign Relations, 1874,* p. 1026.

14. Ibid., pp. 1016, 1021.

15. Ibid., p. 1048.

16. Bliss to Fish, Nov. 28, 1873, Fish Papers.

17. Williams to Fish, Dec. 17, *Foreign Relations, 1874,* pp.1113-15; Fish diary, Dec. 12.

18. Fish to Polo, Dec. 22, *Foreign Relations, 1874,* p. 1051.

19. Attorney General Williams, Dec. 17, 1873, *Foreign Relations, 1874,* p. 1113.

20. Hall to Davis, Dec. 10, Dispatches/Havana.

21. Credit must be given to Castelar who insisted Jovellar obey orders, pointing out that all of the United States arguments were based on the fact Spain did not control Cuba. "Do not mention resignation while the orders of the government are not fulfilled." Cited in Herminio Portell Vilá, *Historia de Cuba, 1853-1878,* 2: 447-48. Jovellar turned down an offer by the Volunteers to support him in resisting giving up the *Virginius;* Crawford to Granville, Dec. 8, F.O. 72/1638; Crawford to Layard, Dec. 15, Layard Papers, Vol. 74.

22. Hall to Davis, Dec. 10, Dispatches/Havana.

23. Hall to Davis, Dec. 13, 1873, Dispatches/Havana.

24. This account of the *Virginius's* departure is from the *New York Times,* Dec. 21, 1873; also Crawford to Layard, Dec. 15, Layard Papers, Vol. 74.

25. Hall to Davis, Dec. 20, Dispatches/Havana. "Would to Heaven that before we had been obliged to suffer. . . that the ire of God and of country may fall forever upon the government which, calling itself Spanish, has done naught else but work out our destruction by its weakness. *A crime which God cannot forgive nor history forget!"* (Pamphlet's italics).

26. Hall to Davis, Dec. 13, *Foreign Relations, 1874,* p. 1091.

27. Lowry to Burriel, Dec. 20, Letters Received by Secretary of the Navy Robeson from Squadron Commanders, Jan. 3 to April 27, 1874, National Archives.

28. Burriel to Lowry, Dec. 20, Robeson letters.

29. Lowry to Burriel, Dec. 21, Robeson letters.
30. Burriel to Lowry, Dec. 22, Robeson letters.
31. Lowry to Burriel, Dec. 22, Robeson letters.
32. Crawford to Granville, Dec. 11, F.O. 72/1638. Statement of Simon Gratz and Henry Canals, Correspondence Relating to the Seizure of the *Virginius*.
33. Ibid.
34. Statement of Henry Canals, Correspondence Relating to the Seizure of the *Virginius*.
35. *New York Times*, Dec. 8.
36. Crawford to Granville, Dec. 7, F.O. 72/1638.
37. *New York Times*, Dec. 19.
38. *New York Times*, Dec. 31, 1873 and Jan. 6, 1874; E.M. Archibald, British Consul, New York, to Thornton, Jan. 23, 1874, F.O. 72/1639.

Chapter Nine

1. Scott to Whiting, Dec. 14, 1873, *Foreign Relations, 1875*, 2:1144. *New York Tribune*, Dec. 18, 1873. Moses P. Handy of the *Tribune* "scooped" other reporters on the return of the vessel. No other newspaper had a reporter at the scene. See Moses P. Handy, "A Special Correspondent's Story," *Lippincott's Monthly Magazine*, 50 (Dec., 1892): 757-65.
2. *New York Tribune*, Dec. 18, 1873; Whiting to Scott, Dec. 17, *Foreign Relations, 1875*, 2:1144-45.
3. *New York Tribune*, Dec. 18, 1873; Moses Handy, "A Special Correspondent's Story," p. 763.
4. *New York Tribune*, Dec. 18, *Foreign Relations, 1875*, 2:1145.
5. *New York Tribune*, Dec. 18.
6. Ibid.
7. Ibid.
8. E.B. Underwood, "An International Incident," *United States Naval Institute Proceedings*, 51 (Jan., 1925): 87.
9. This and subsequent information from ibid., pp. 87-90 and Woodrow to Robeson, *Foreign Relations, 1875*, pp. 1145-46.

Chapter Ten

1. Benjamin Moran's Journal, Dec. 8, 1873.
2. Sickles to Fish, Dec. 6, *Foreign Relations, 1874*, p. 973.
3. The *Atlanta Constitution* on Nov. 30 editorialized after the protocol's publication that it was obvious negotiations had been taken out of Sickles's hands. Any problems, it believed, were due to Sickles's

bungling since Castelar had been ready to settle from the start.

4. Layard Memoirs, III, p. 70.

5. Ibid.; Swanberg, *Sickles the Incredible*, pp. 349-50.

6. Layard to Granville, Dec. 7, F.O. 72/1638.

7. Fish to Sickles, Dec. 6, *Foreign Relations, 1874*, p. 973.

8. Swanberg, *Sickles the Incredible*, p. 949.

9. *New York Herald,* Dec. 3.

10. Thornton to Granville, Jan. 5, 1874, F.O. 72/1639.

11. Sickles to Fish, Dec. 6, 1873, *Foreign Relations, 1874*, p. 973.

12. Fish to Sickles, Dec. 17, ibid., p. 974.

13. Sickles to Fish, Dec. 20, ibid., p. 975.

14. Thornton to Granville, Jan. 26, 1874, F.O. 72/1629.

15. Quoted in Swanberg, *Sickles the Incredible*, p. 350.

16. *The Nation*, 17 (Dec. 11, 1873): 378.

17. *New York Tribune*, Dec. 8, 1873.

18. Sickles to Fish, Dec. 26, *Foreign Relations, 1874*, p. 975.

19. Sickles to Fish, Dec. 21, Dispatches/Spain; Swanberg, *Sickles the Incredible*, p. 350.

20. Strobel, *The Spanish Revolution*, pp. 230-32.

21. Ibid., p. 232.

22. Emilio Castelar, *Discursos Intigros Pronunciados en las Córtes Constituyentes de 1873-1874* (Barcelone, 1874), p. 219.

23. Ibid.; Trend, *The Origins of Modern Spain*, p. 29.

24. Castelar, *Discursos Intigros Pronunciados en las Córtes Constituyentes*, pp. 222-37.

25. Castelar's final speech, "I protest with all my soul against the disruption of the Cortes," is certainly his shortest but one of his best, ibid., p. 238. The account of the fall of the republic is from Strobel, *Spanish Revolution*, pp. 232-37; Trend, *The Origins of Modern Spain*, pp. 28-29; Brandt, *Toward the New Spain*, p. 326.

26. Layard to Granville, private, Jan. 3, 1874, Layard Papers, vol. 195.

27. Raymond Carr, *Spain, 1808-1939*, p. 330; more realistic was the writer in *The Nation* who wrote "No, 'Spanish republic' has been overthrown, because none existed," "The Latest Revolution in Spain," *The Nation*, 17 (Jan, 8, 1874): 20.

28. Cushing to Evarts, Jan. 5, 1874, Cushing Papers, Library of Congress.

29. Fish to Grant, Dec. 22, 1874, Fish Papers. Fish also told Polo that Cushing's nomination showed the class of person the United States wanted to represent it in Spain; Polo to Minister of State, Jan. 12, 1874, Correspondencia, Embajadas y Legaciones, EE Unidos, 1873-1875, Leg. 1474.

(159)

30. Claude M. Fuess, *The Life of Caleb Cushing,* 2 vols. (New York: Harcourt, Brace & Co., 1923), 2:364-65. The label of shiftiness in politics hurt Cushing. James Russell Lowell's *Bigelow Papers* satirized him:

> General C. is a deffle smart man;
> He's ben on all side that give places of pelf;
> But consistency still wuz a part of his plan, —
> He's ben true to one part and that is himself.

31. Because of his pronounced sympathy with Spain, Cushing was *persona grata.* Admiral Polo told Fish it was "very urgent" that Cushing be appointed, and expressed confidence that it would produce good effect, Fish diary, Jan. 15, 1874; Thornton believed Polo wanted Fish to tell Cushing to do as little as possible and "follow up his own tastes of diving into old Spanish archives;" Thornton to Tenterden, Feb. 3, 1874, Lord Tenterden Papers, vol. 4, F.O. 363/4; Polo to Minister of State, Feb. 16, 1874, Correspondencia/E. E. Unidos, Leg. 1474.

32. N. Paige to Cushing, Jan. 15, 1874, Cushing Papers.

33. Fuess, *The Life of Caleb Cushing,* 2:379.

34. Cushing to Fish, April 9, Cushing Papers.

35. Layard, who later became close friends with Cushing, noted the Spaniards could never understand whether he postponed presenting his credentials through ignorance or contempt for diplomatic formalities. While waiting he allowed himself to be entertained at a public dinner by an American dentist and met members of the Republican party and opponents of the government which immediately caused offense to the ministry, Layard Memoirs, III, p. 122.

36. Ibid., p. 123.

37. Ibid.

38. Cushing to Fish, July 5, Cushing Papers.

39. Layard to Derby, June 19, F.O. 72/1640.

40. Ibid.

41. H.G. McDonnel, Acting Consul/Madrid, to Derby, Aug. 10 and Aug. 19 F.O. 72/1640.

42. Fish diary, June 19; Cushing to Fish, June 22; Polo and Fish parted on the best of terms.

43. Layard to Derby, Oct. 23, F.O. 72/1640; Layard to Derby, confidential, Nov. 24, F.O. 72/1640.

44. Fish diary, Nov. 19.

45. Ibid., Nov. 21.

46. Ibid., Dec. 25.

47. Fish to Cushing, Nov. 28, *Foreign Relations, 1875,* II, p. 1236.

48. Layard Memoirs, III, pp. 147-48; Cushing to Fish, Jan. 15,

Cushing Papers.

49. Cushing to Fish, Jan. 20, 1875, Cushing Papers; perhaps Castro interpreted Cushing's comparison as a veiled threat.

50. Cushing to Castro, Jan. 26, Cushing Papers.

51. Cushing to Fish, Jan. 26, ibid.

52. Cushing to Fish, Feb. 8, ibid; Cushing to Castro, Feb. 11, ibid.

53. The interview with Castro is recorded in Cushing to Fish, Feb. 21; Cushing thought his historical analogies during his presentation to the king made a very favorable impression. *La Epoca*, March 12, commented that the American minister had already shown himself at ease with the Spanish language and literature, "but this minister goes further in his discourse, for he calls up the glories of the Spanish monarchy," clipping in Cushing Papers.

54. Fish diary, Nov. 19, 1874; Spain had with better reason rewarded Captain Costilla and the crew of the *Tornado,* Layard to Derby, private, June 9, 1874, Layard Papers, vol. 195.

55. Cushing to Ulloa, Nov. 30, 1874, Cushing Papers.

56. Cushing to Fish, Feb. 1 and Feb. 4, 1874, ibid.

57. Cushing to Fish, Feb. 1, 1875, ibid.

58. Cushing to Fish, Oct. 9, 1875, ibid. During a visit to Bilbao, where Burriel commanded troops, Layard refused to receive the general; Burriel complained about the Englishman's "outrageous" behavior, but Layard answered he would not meet an "assassin" who had not been brought to justice, Waterfield, *Layard of Nineveh,* p. 345.

59. Cushing to Conde Casa-Valencia, Nov. 10, 1875, Cushing Papers; Cushing was sympathetic to Spanish legal delays pointing out to Fish that the United Sates had similar cases of procrastination, April 12, 1876, *Foreign Relations, 1876,* p. 530. The Spanish found it no less exasperating that Sir Lambton Loraine was regarded as a hero in America and given a testimonial dinner in New York. Several news clippings of this are included in Polo to Minister of State, April 29, 1874, Correspondencia/E.E. Unidos, Leg. 1474.

60. Chadwick, *Relations of the United States and Spain,* 1:353.

61. Cushing to Fish, Feb. 9 and Feb. 22, 1877, Cushing Papers.

62. Chadwick, *Relations of the United States and Spain,* 1:353, n. 3.

Chapter Eleven

1. Charles Cheney Hyde, *International Law Chiefly as Interpreted and Applied by the United States,* 2 vols. (Boston: Little Brown, 1951) 1:774.

2. H. Lauterpacht, ed., L. Oppenheim, *International Law, A Treatise,* 2 vols. (New York: Longmans, Green, 1967) 1:608.

3. Ellery C. Stowell and Henry F. Munro, *International Cases:*

Peace, 1 (Boston: Houghton Miflin, 1916), p. 370.

4. John Bassett Moore, *A Digest of International Law,* 2 (Washington, D.C.: U.S. Gov't P.O.): 981.

5. William Edward Hall, *A Treatise on International Law* (Oxford: Oxford University Press, 1909), p. 262.

6. George Boutwell to Grant, Dec. 24, 1873, New York Historical Society, Mics. Ms. B.

7. H. Lauterpacht, editor, L. Oppenheim, *International Law,* 1:301, n. 1.

8. Stowell and Munro, *International Cases: Peace,* 1:371.

9. James Brown Scott, *Cases on International Law* (Boston: Boston Book Co., 1902), pp. 320-22.

10. Cited in Moore, *Digest of International Law,* 2:981.

11. Cited in Edwin Borchard and William Potter Lage, *Neutrality for the United States* (New Haven: Yale University Press, 1940), p. 178, n. 2.

12. George Ticknor Curtis, *The Case of the Virginius* (New York, 1874), pp. 39-40.

13. Hall, *A Treatise on International Law,* p. 262.

14. Hyde, *International Law,* 2:245.

15. Curtis, *Case of the Virginius,* pp. 39-40. In January, 1877 Spain and the United States signed a protocol which prohibited the executive authority on Cuba from arresting and detaining American citizens without trial. The two governments agreed that the protocol's provisions would not be binding if men were "captured with arms in hand;" Moore, *Digest of International Law,* 2:197.

16. *New York Times,* Nov. 24, 1873.

17. Richard Hofstadter was one of the first scholars to offer a brief comparison of conditions in the seventies and nineties in "Cuba, the Philippines and Manifest Destiny," *The Paranoid Style in American Politics and Other Essays* (New York: A.A. Knopf, 1965), p. 151, n. 2. The best comparison is in James B. Chapin, "Hamilton Fish and the lessons of the Ten Year's War," *Perspectives in American Diplomacy* (New York, 1976), pp. 131-63.

18. See the *New York Times,* Nov. 28, 1873 for its attack on the *Herald* because of its "bogus" news; Royal Cortissoz, *The Life of Whitelaw Reid,* 1 (New York: Scribner's, 1921): 263; Reid to Fish, Dec. 29, Reid Papers, Library of Congress.

19. As William Cullen Bryant wrote Fish, "We do not want Cuba, with her ignorant population of Negroes, mulattos. . . alien to our own population;" Bryant to Fish, Nov. 19, 1873, Fish Papers; Nevins, *Hamilton Fish,* p. 47.

20. William McKinley, a man not unlike Fish, opposed annexing Cuba, because he did not want the problem of assimilating an alien

society. Walter LaFeber, "That 'Splendid Little War': An Historical Perspective," *The Texas Quarterly* 11 (Winter, 1968): 89-98. Yet he favored annexing the no less alien Philippines. See Christopher Lasch, "The Anti-Imperialists, the Philippines, and the Inequality of Man," *Journal of Southern History,* 14 (Aug., 1958): 319-31.

21. Few took the cold-eyed view of *The Nation* that Spain had changed the name, not the substance of its politics, and the republic "left Spain just as she was, neither better nor worse; the defects of character, and manners and opinions which had made her for a century and a half a declining nation were still as deep as ever." "The Reasons for Keeping Cool About It," *The Nation* 17 (November 20, 1873): 334. Both the Fish and Sumner papers have several letters from people who believed war with the United States would end the Spanish republic.

22. Badeau, *Grant in Peace,* p. 232.

23. Nevins, *Hamilton Fish,* p. 907.

24. Vilá, *Historia de Cuba, 1853-1878,* 2:452. Also, James B. Chapin's critical assessment, "Hamilton Fish and American Expansion" in Frank Merli and Theodore Wilson, *Makers of American Diplomacy,* 1 (New York, 1974): 223-51, based on his doctoral dissertation.

25. Nevins, *Hamilton Fish,* p. 694.

26. Interview with General William T. Sherman, *National Republican,* Nov. 17, 1873.

27. "How Should We Fight Spain?" *The Nation* 17 (Dec. 4, 1873): 364; Lawrence Carroll Allin, "The First Cuban War—The *Virginius* Affair," *American Neptune,* 38 (Oct., 1978): 233-48 is good on naval affairs for the period.

28. Robley D. Evans, *A Sailor's Log, Recollections of Forty Years of Naval Life* (New York: D. Appleton & Co., 1901), p. 171.

29. See the account by Harold and Margaret Sprout, *The Rise of American Naval Power* (Princeton: Princeton University Press, 1967), pp. 183-201; Peter Karsten, *The Naval Aristocracy, the Golden Age of Annapolis and the Emergence of Modern American Navalism* (New York: Free Press, 1972), passim. Kenneth J. Hagan, "The Impact of the *Virginius* Crisis Upon American Foreign and Naval Policy," unpublished paper in possession of author.

30. Geoffrey Blainey, *The Causes of War* (New York: MacMillan, 1973), pp. 87-90, has an interesting discussion of the topic.

31. As Foner states the case, to leave the "economic production in the western provinces untouched was to fight the Spanish with one hand tied behind one's back," *A History of Cuba,* 2:228.

32. The best analysis of American economic expansion is Walter LaFeber, *The New Empire: An Interpretation of American Expansion,*

1860-1898 (Ithaca: Cornell University Press, 1963).

33. Cuban sugar exports fell by over 50% during the first year of the war and by 75% by 1898. Philip S. Foner, *The Spanish-Cuban-American War and the Birth of American Imperialism, 1845-1898,* (New York: International Pub., 1972), pp. 106-07; LaFeber, *The New Empire,* p. 38 and Foner, *A History of Cuba,* 2:296-97, detail the growth of American investments.

34. The classic statement of this argument is Alec Lawrence Macfie's "The Outbreak of War and the Trade Cycle," *Economic History* 3 (Feb., 1938): 89-97. It is skillfully recounted in Blainey, *The Causes of War,* pp. 91-96 and in the notes, pp. 256-57.

35. See the interesting article by Tennant S. McWilliams, "Procrastination Diplomacy: Hannis Taylor and the Cuban Business Disputes, 1893-97," *Diplomatic History* 2 (Winter, 1978): 63-80.

36. Hugh Thomas, *Cuba, the Pursuit of Freedom* (New York: Harper & Row, 1971), p. 266; Philip Foner, *A History of Cuba* 2, Chapter 21, passim.

37. Fish diary, June 19, 1874.

38. Ryan proved to be a Canadian who in spite of Union service never claimed United States citizenship. He was not included in the reparation payments by Spain to the United States, nor did Fish show interest in his rather special case. Fish diary, Jan. 13, 1876, entry by Assistant Secretary of State John Cadwalader.

39. Sickles to James M. Callahan, June 5, 1899, quoted in Callahan, *Cuba and International Relations* (Baltimore: Johns Hopkins University Press, 1899), p. 410.

40. Nevins, *Hamilton Fish,* pp. 888-905.

41. Nevins, *Hamilton Fish,* p. 916. Edmund Morris, *The Rise of Theodore Roosevelt* (New York: Coward, McCann and Geoghegan, 1979) p. 643.

Note On Sources

I. ARCHIVAL COLLECTIONS

United States:

The Hamilton Fish Papers in the Manuscript Division of the Library of Congress, Washington, D.C., consist of dozens of containers of Fish's correspondence. They include the voluminous diary kept while secretary of state. Hermino Portell Vilá is correct in saying that the Fish diary is not a diary only, if one thinks that a person must confide his innermost thoughts to secret books. Fish carefully noted what happened in the routine of public life—arguments, counterarguments, appointments, disappointments but seldom gave vent to opinion. The present writer believes that the public man seldom differed from the private one, and that the diary is highly reliable. Indispensable as a source on diplomacy, the diary shows Fish rarely ventured into domestic politics and it would be disappointing to the historian approaching it from that perspective.

Fish's reticence in discussing personalities was not shared by Benjamin Moran, clerk of the American legation in London. His journals, also in the Library of Congress, make interesting reading. Moran has some valuable comments on the elusive Daniel Sickles's conduct in Madrid, and was one of the few individuals Sickles corresponded with.

The Elihu Washburne papers have a few letters on the *Virginius* affair and on Sickles. As our minister to France, Washburne was perhaps the ablest American representative abroad during the Grant years.

There is nothing regarding the *Virginius* in the Ulysses S. Grant collection except letters from military units offering their services in the event of a war with Spain.

The William M. Evarts manuscripts have nothing on the subject.

James G. Garfield's collection briefly offers one important congressman's view of the crisis between Spain and the United States. Unfortunately it says little of fellow congressmen's attitudes.

Daniel Sickles's papers in the Library of Congress are sketchy and deal mainly with the Civil War years. His papers in the New York Historical Society collection are more extensive and contain fascinating pieces, such as the letter which disclosed his wife's adultery and led to the murder of Philip Barton Key. Unfortunately, most of his papers were destroyed in a fire in 1885. One can imagine Sickles

(165)

feeding the flames with incriminating documents.

Alvey A. Adee destroyed his papers before his death in 1924, and his family papers in the Library of Congress contain little of value. But the John Russell Young Papers, also in the Library of Congress, include a couple of interesting letters from Adee concerning the *Virginius* affair.

The papers of Charles Sumner are in the Widener Library, Harvard University. They are interesting and complete on his views of Spanish-American relations and also on letters from the public expressing attitudes pro and con to Sumner's stand on the Cuban question.

Great Britain:

Exceeding even Hamilton Fish's Papers in importance for understanding of how the crisis was resolved are the papers of Sir Austin Henry Layard, British minister to Spain, now located in the Manuscript Division of the British Museum. The papers are owned by The Right Honorable, the Viscount Wimborne, and permission is necessary for examination. Layard's unpublished memoirs are in the collection. A brilliant and opinionated diplomat, he wrote letters and memoirs that make good reading.

The private papers of William E. Gladstone, prime minister during the *Virginius* episode, are in the British Museum. Scattered through them are some letters from Lord Clarendon, foreign secretary, which are interesting for the early years of the trouble with Spain. Clarendon died in 1870. Generally, however, the Gladstone papers contain little of significance for the subject. The same holds for the Cabinet papers also in the British Museum.

The Public Record Office has collections of Lord Granville, foreign secretary, and of Lord Tenterden, permanent under-secretary. The papers have a few items of interest.

The P.R.O. also houses the Foreign Office papers. Much but not all of the voluminous correspondence regarding the *Virginius* seizure as it affected the British government is collected in four volumes, F.O. 72/1637—F.O. 72/1640. While the student needs a pass to work in the P.R.O., once he gains admittance there are no restrictions on papers dealing with this period.

Spain:

The Foreign Ministry building in Madrid contains archives of the Ministry (Archive del Ministeriode Asuntos Exteriores). For admittance one must have a letter of introduction, usually obtainable at the

American Embassy. In spite of the imposing appearance of rifle-bearing guards at entrances to the Ministry, the researcher once inside finds the archival employees are extremely helpful. The subterranean location of the manuscripts is particularly welcome to refugees from Madrid's stiffling summer heat. All documents in the archives down to 1931 are open to scholars. The slim and unorganized correspondence dealing with the *Virginius* is, like most of the manuscripts, tied in bundles (legajos) under Correspondencis Embajadoras Y. Elgaciones EE Unidos, Legajos 1473 and 1474 dealing with the years 1873-1875.

II. GOVERNMENT PUBLICATIONS

The National Archives diplomatic (RG 59) and Naval (RG 45) collections are on microfilm, obtainable upon purchase from the archives. The most important documents relating to the *Virginius* are in appropriate volumes of *Foreign Relations of the United States* (Washington, 1874-1876).

The English equivalent of *Foreign Relations* is *British and Foreign State Papers, 1873-1874* (London, 1881), which is less complete than the American series.

There is no equivalent publication by the Spanish government covering the *Virginius* episode.

III. BIOGRAPHIES AND AUTOBIOGRAPHIES

Allan Nevins's *Hamilton Fish: The Inner History of the Grant Administration* (New York: Dodd, Mead & Co., 1937) won the Pulitzer Prize and is one of the great biographies of American statesmen. Nevins's account of the *Virginius* is exclusively from Fish's perspective and gives the secretary more credit for the peaceful settlement than he deserves. He pays little attention to pressures of Spanish politics and says nothing of Layard's role. It remains valuable both as history and literature, for analysis of Fish's character and relations with the Grant administration.

The account by Joseph V. Fuller, "Hamilton Fish," in Samuel Flagg Bemis, ed., *The American Secretaries of State and Their Diplomacy*, 7 (New York: A.A. Knopf, 1928), pp. 125-214 is still worth attention.

Fish's antagonist, Sickles, is the subject of a lively biography by W. A. Swanberg, *Sickles the Incredible* (New York: Scribners, 1956). Due to the lack of any extensive papers it is unlikely that anyone will surpass Swanberg's account, either for scholarship or readability.

William B. Hesseltine, *Ulysses S. Grant, Politician* (New York: Dodd, Mead & Co., 1935) is the best book on Grant's presidential years.

Hesseltine is too kind to Grant's political career. A new book on Grant the president is sorely needed. See also the old work by Grant's secretary, Adam Badeau, *Grant in Peace* (Hartford: S.S. Scranton, 1887) which gives an intimate portrait.

Expansionists of the Grant administration are covered in Fred Harvey Harrington's *Fighting Politician, Major General N. P. Banks* (Philadelphia: University of Pennsylvania Press, 1948). Banks's career in the House was cut short by the election of 1872. James H. Wilson published the life and letters of the most important early influence in Grant's presidency in *The Life of John A. Rawlins* (New York: Neale Publishing Co., 1916). Death removed this source of trouble for Fish, but for nearly a century afterward Rawlins was the most popular North American to Cubans.

Fish's sometime ally, later an enemy, Charles Sumner, perhaps one of the most disliked men in American history, has an admirable biographer in David Donald, *Charles Sumner and the Rights of Man* (New York: A.A. Knopf, 1970), a volume which does full justice to the idealistic but irascible Bostonian. It is unlikely that anyone will add more to the life of Sumner's fellow New Englander and political enemy, Caleb Cushing, than appears in Claude M. Fuess's sympathetic *Life of Caleb Cushing*, 2 vols. (New York: Harcourt, Brace & Co., 1923).

An account of the meeting at Steinway Hall is in Brainerd Dyer's *The Public Career of William M. Evarts* (Berkeley: University of California Press, 1933). Royal Cortissoz, *The Life of Whitelaw Reid*, 1 (New York: Scribners, 1921) has information on the *Virginius*. The *New York Tribune* scooped other papers on news of the vessel's surrender. An interesting intellectual biography of a leading critic of the Grant administration is W. M. Armstrong, *E. L. Godkin and American Foreign Policy, 1865-1900* (New York: Bookmen Associates, 1957). The editor of *The Nation* took a cool approach to revolution in both Cuba and Spain.

Some naval commanders of the Gilded Age have told their stories— Robley D. Evans, *A Sailor's Log, Recollection of Forty Years of Naval Life* (New York: D. Appleton & Co., 1901), and Seaton Schroeder, *A Half Century of Naval Service* (New York: D. Appleton & Co., 1922). Evans is more interesting, as he tells of service on the last of the wooden warships and first of the ironclads, in the days when promotions were slow and budgets low.

The short, unhappy life of Captain Joseph Fry was compiled by a Victorian lady from letters and newspaper accounts, with some information from his family in Jeanie Mort Walker, *Life of Captain Joseph Fry, The Cuban Martyr* (Hartford: J. B. Burr Publishing Co., 1875).

The captain was an interesting fellow who deserved a better book.

The British minister in Madrid, Layard, has an interesting biographer in Gordon Waterfield, *Layard of Nineveh* (New York: Praeger, 1968). Waterfield gives fair coverage of the Spanish Ministry, and also Layard's ambassadorship to Turkey after leaving Spain. If nothing else, he deserves credit for deciphering Layard's cramped handwriting.

Hermino Portell Vilá has written a short, interesting account of the man who directed the first phase of the Ten Years War, *Céspedes: El Padre de la Patria Cubana* (Madrid: Espasa-Calpe, 1931). Lives of generals of the revolution are chronicled in Carlos Manuel de Céspedes y Quesada, *Manual de Quesada y Loynaz* (Habana: Imprinte "El Sigle XX", 1925), and a dissertation at Duke finished in 1954, Lawrence R. Nichols, "The Bronze Titan, The Mulatto Hero of Cuban Independence, Antonio Maceo." Nichols's study uses Cuban sources and was completed when scholars could still use the Cuban archives. It would be interesting if some student would make a study of such American military advisers in the Cuban army as Ryan and Thomas Jordan.

The fullest account of the great liberal statesman Castelar is Manuel Gonzales Araco, *Castelar, Su Vida y Su Muerte* (Madrid, 1900). For the only work in English see David Hannay, *Don Emilio Castelar* (London: Sands and Foster, 1896). A prolific writer of biographies, Hannay had lived in Spain during Castelar's administration when his father was British consul in Cartagena. Alvey A. Adee, "Reminiscences of Castelar," *Century Magazine*, N.S. 9 (March, 1886), pp. 792-94 has many interesting and novel points by an astute observer of men, as does his "A Prefatory Note on Spanish Politics," *Century Magazine*, N.S. 35 (Nov., 1898), pp. 140-42. C. A. M. Hennessy, *Pi y Margall and the Federal Republican Movement, 1868-1874* (Oxford: Clarendon Press, 1962) is the most recent work on the era of republican experiment but is disappointingly brief on Castelar. The latter's administration is in Conde de Romanones, *Los Cuarto Presidentes de la Primera República Española* (Espasa-Calph, S.A., 1939).

IV. GENERAL WORKS

A good starting point for Latin American relations is Samuel Flagg Bemis, *The Latin American Policy of the United States* (New York: Harcourt, Brace & Co., 1943). The dean of American diplomatic historians gives a nationalist's view of relations south of the border, refuting many criticisms made of the United States. J. Lloyd Mecham provides a political scientist's background in *A Survey of United States-Latin*

American Relations (Boston: Houghton Mifflin, 1965), a topical ac-count. Lester D. Langley, *The Cuban Policy of the United States: A Brief History* (New York: Wiley, 1968) is an excellent survey. A work on American policy during the Ten Years War would be welcome.

Decisions for peace or war between nations are often based on feelings much older than participants realize. American attitudes to-ward Spain were formed as early as the sixteenth and seventeenth centuries. For analysis of ideas which influenced Americans with regard to both Spain and Cuba see James W. Cortada's *Two Nations Over Time: Spain and the United States, 1776-1977* (Westport, Conn.: Greenwood Press, 1978); also Philip Wayne Powell, *Tree of Hate: Propaganda and Prejudices Affecting United States Relations with the Hispanic World* (New York: Basic Books, 1971). The same theme is pursued in a volume edited by Charles Gibson, *The Black Legend, Anti-Spanish Attitudes in the Old World and the New* (New York: A.A. Knopf, 1971). Economic relations between Cuba and the United States appear in Roland T. Ely, "The Old Cuba Trade: Highlights and Case Studies of Cuban-American Interdependence During the Nineteenth Century," *Business History Review,* 38 (Winter, 1964): 456-78. Basil Rauch, *American Interest in Cuba, 1848-1855* (New York: Columbia University Press, 1948) provides much detail, and Clifford L. Egan, "Cuba, Spain and the American Civil War," *Rocky Mountain Social Science Journal,* 5 (1968): 58-63 is important.

In the extensive literature dealing with Cuba and the United States the old volumes by James M. Callahan, *Cuba and International Rela-tions* (Baltimore: Johns Hopkins University Press, 1899), and French E. Chadwick, *The Relations of the United States and Spain,* 1 (New York: Scribners, 1909) are still valuable. Chadwick was an admiral in the United States navy who like many seafaring men made a solid contribution to American historical writing. Philip S. Foner, *A History of Cuba and Its Relations with the United States, 1492-1845,* 1 (New York: International Publishers, 1962) and *1845-1895,* 2 (New York, 1963) is a Marxist approach which relies on Portell. Although it has been criticized it is a moderate, believable account on the subject, the most thorough in English. A mammoth work by the British scholar Hugh Thomas, *Cuba, The Pursuit of Freedom* (New York: Harper & Row, 1971) has good coverage of Spanish politics during the repub-lican period. Thomas avoids the biases that often creep into American Cuban writings.

For background to American diplomacy in the Gilded Age see the book in the New American Nation series by Charles S. Campbell, *The Transformation of American Foreign Relations, 1865-1900* (New York: Harper & Row, 1976) and Robert L. Beisner, *From the Old*

Diplomacy to the New, 1865-1900 (New York: Crowell, 1975) which is an interesting interpretive study. Also see Milton Plesur, *America's Outward Thrust: Approaches to Foreign Affairs, 1865-1890* (De Kalb, Ill.: Northern Illinois University Press, 1971) and Foster R. Dulles, *Prelude to World Power: American Diplomatic History, 1869-1900* (New York: MacMillan, 1965). Ernest R. May, *American Imperialism: An Interpretive Essay* (New York: Atheneum, 1969) touches the expansion during the 1870s, using public opinion techniques. Walter LaFeber's *The New Empire: An Interpretation of American Expansion, 1860-1898* (Ithaca, N.Y.: Cornell University Press, 1963) looks at economic influences in foreign policy, with a controversial thesis that the latter decades of the nineteenth century marked a constant search for markets. Donald M. Dozer, "Anti-Imperialism in the United States, 1865-1898," an unpublished dissertation, Harvard, 1936, focuses on opponents of expansion, as does the article by Robert L. Beisner, "Thirty Year Before Manila: E. L. Godkin, Carl Schurz, and Anti-Imperialism in the Gilded Age," *Historian*, 30 (1968): 561-77.

The place to begin any study of Cuban-American relations from the Cuban point of view is Hermino Portell Vilá, *Historia de Cuba en Sus Relaciones con los Estados Unidos y España, 1853-1898*, 2 (Habana: J. Montero, 1939). Portell is a Cuban nationalist, somewhat similar to Bemis in the United States. He attacks elements within the revolution who considered annexation to the United States, but criticizes the American government for not intervening to help the revolutionists. He dismisses Secretary Fish for holding back only because he, Fish, believed Cuba would eventually fall into the hands of the United States without war, in spite of Fish's perhaps unnoble but realistic statements that he did not want to add Cuba's race problems to those that already perplexed the nation.

For Cuba's domestic affairs see Arthur F. Corwin, *Spain and the Abolition of Slavery in Cuba, 1817-1886* (Austin: University of Texas Press, 1967) a first-rate study. Franklin W. Knight, *Slave Society in Cuba During the Nineteenth Century* (Madison: University of Wisconsin Press, 1970) presents a different view of reasons for emancipation; the author is a native of the West Indies. Finally there is the classic study by Fernando Ortiz, *Cuban Counterpoint: Tobacco*, trans. by Harriet De Onís (New York: A.A. Knopf, 1947). Cuban works include Francisco J. Ponte Dominguez, *Historia de la Guerra de los Diez Años, Desde Su Origin Hasta la Asambea de Guaimaro*, 1 (Habana, 1944) for early years of the revolution; Ramiro Guerra y Sánchez, *Guerra de los Diez Años, 1868-1878* (Habana: Imprinte "El Sigle XX," 1950) a social interpretation. One of the most interesting contemporary volumes about the island is an 1870 travel guide by

Samuel Hazard, *Cuba With Pen and Pencil* (Hartford: Hartford Publishing Co., 1871), an extremely clear picture of day-to-day life, food, lodging, entertainment, prices. See also A. Gallenga, *The Pearl of the Antilles* (London: Chapman & Hall, 1873), by a London *Times* correspondent reprinted in 1970.

Spanish accounts pertaining to the revolt are Justo Zaragoza, *Las Insurrecciones en Cuba, Apuntes Para la Historia Politica de Esta Isla en Presente Siglo* (Madrid: M.G. Hernandez, 1872-73), a defense of actions of the Volunteers by one of their officers, and D. Ildefonso Antiono Bermejo, *Historia de la Interinidad y Guerra Civil de España Desde 1868,* 3 (Madrid: R. Labajos, 1877), which provides a wealth of material on Spain during the troubled republican years. It is particularly important for reproducing cables to the government at the time of the *Virginius* seizure. For good coverage of Spanish foreign relations see the work of Jerónimo Bécker, *Historia de las Relaciones Exteriores de España Durante el Sigle XIX, 1868-1900,* 3 (Madrid: J. Ratés, 1926). Bécker was an archivist who during the early years of this century wrote several volumes on his country's foreign policy. International ramifications of the Spanish revolution are explored by William A. Smith, "The European Powers and the Spanish Revolution, 1868-1875," unpublished dissertation, Harvard, 1946; in spite of the title this study concentrates on the years to 1871, and sketches later developments. Older accounts of the Spanish revolution are Joseph A. Brandt, *Toward the New Spain* (Chicago: University of Chicago Press, 1933) and J. B. Trend, *Origins of Modern Spain* (New York: Russell and Russell, 1965). An account by an American diplomat who served in Spain is Edward Henry Strobel, *The Spanish Revolution, 1868-1875* (Boston: Small, Maynard & Co, 1898).

V. ARTICLES

Valuable articles on the *Virginius* affair are by Rudolph de Cordova, "The *Virginius* Incident and Cuba," *Nineteenth Century,* 60 (Dec., 1906): 976-85, and E. B. Underwood, "An International Incident," *United States Naval Institute Proceedings,* 51 (1925): 83-90. Before America's entrance into the First World War the incident was the subject of articles by authors trying to draw parallels with the submarine problem of 1914-17—for which see Burton M. Hendrick, "Historic Crises in American Diplomacy," *The World's Work,* 32 (June, 1916): 179-86; S. G. Lapham, "Commander Cushing and the *Virginius,*" *Americana,* 10 (Oct., 1915): 903-05; "When Americans Demanded War in Vain," *Literary Digest,* 52 (June, 1916): 1802-06; and most interestingly the account in "*Virginius* and the *Lusitania:* a Comparison," *Outlook,* 112 (April, 1916): 770-71.

VI. NEWSPAPERS

Newspapers proved of mixed value for the present study. The *New York Herald* is amusing because it served as Sickles's mouthpiece and was an early example of yellow journalism, also because it was always so wrong about what was happening or what the mood of the country seemed to be. What would today be called "establishment" papers, the *New York Times* and the *New York Tribune,* both worked with Fish and supported his position on the *Virginius.* Sir Edward Thornton believed that Fish used the Washington *National Republican* to advertise his policies, but that seems unlikely in view of the problems that journal caused him. The *New York World* was an example of a Democratic paper that generally supported Fish's Cuban policy and had no use for the former Democrat, Sickles. The *Chicago Tribune, Boston Daily Globe, Philadelphia Inquirer, Savannah News,* and *Richmond Whig* were representative of their sections and politics. The *New Orleans Picayune* was particularly interesting because of that city's long association with filibusters.

British newspapers had surprisingly little to say of the *Virginius* affair, other than comments on America's position. The *London Times* provided the most adequate coverage.

Spanish newspapers united in condemning American meddling in the affairs of Cuba.

VII. BIBLIOGRAPHICAL AIDS

Perhaps most useful for study of the *Virginius* was David R. Trask, et al., *A Bibliography of United States-Latin American Relations Since 1810* (Lincoln: University of Nebraska Press, 1968). Although now in need of updating Samuel Flagg Bemis and Grace G. Griffin, *Guide to the Diplomatic History of the United States: 1775-1921* (Washington: U.S. Government Printing Office, 1935) is still helpful. An indispensable aid for locating manuscripts is *National Union Catalog of Manuscript Collections* (Washington, 1962--). Eric H. Boehm, ed., *America: History and Life* (Santa Barbara: A.B.C. Clio, 1964) provides assistance for journal articles.

(173)

Index

Adee, Alvey Augustus, 21
Alabama claims, 15
Alfonso, King of Spain: assumes Spanish throne, 125; negotiations for reparations, 126; punishment of Burriel, 127
Amadeo I, King of Spain, 21, 22
Army, U.S., 69
Atlas, S.S., 31, 33, 37
Autran, José Maria: prosecutor at captives' trial, 51; *Virginius's* right to fly U.S. flag, 29-30

Babcock, Orville, 92
Bancroft, George, 87
Banks, Nathaniel P., 13
Baynard, William, 35
Bazan, 29, 30, 31, 106
Beecher, Henry Ward, 15, 71
Bell, Charles, 52
Bembetta: background, 33; directs Cuban expedition, 37; execution, 46-47; paraded in Santiago, 44; reaction to pursuit by *Tornado,* 40-41; tried and sentenced, 45
Bennett, James Gordon, 63
Bennett, James Gordon, Jr., 64, 65
Billy Butts, 26
Black Legend, 13
Blanco, Guzman, 26, 27
Bliss, George, 100, 101
Boutwell, George, 130
Bowen, Francis, 27, 100-01
Brady, Edwin L., 88
Braine, D.L., 106, 107
Brequa, Sanchez, 75, 120
Brooks, Theodore: and *Virginius* prisoners, 47-48; lodges protests with Burriel, 49, 54; receives cable from John P. Grant, 49-51; seeks delay of executions, 49

Bryant, William Cullen, 63
Buchanan, James, 6, 18
Burke, George, 36
Burriel, Juan D.: advances date of executions, 52; and salute to U.S. flag, 104-05; closes telegraph offices, 45; death, 128; denies John P. Grant's appeal, 51; denies request for delay of executions, 49; meets with Schmitt, 45-46; plans prisoners' execution, 45; promotion, 128; punishment question, 123, 126-28; receives citizens' pleas for mercy, 54; receives Lorraine and Brooks, 54; reports executions to Havana, 47

Cámara, Manuel de la, 110
Cameron, Simon, 97, 132
Campos, Arsenio Martinez, 137
Canals, Henry, 105
Canandaigua, U.S.S., 29, 30
Cartagena, 81
Carvajal, José de: and Spanish press, 84-85; anger with Sickles, 80-81; negotiates with Sickles, 76-85; Thanksgiving protocol, 94
Castelar, Emilio: and Spanish press, 84; appearance, 24; death, 137; elected president of Spain, 24; meets with Layard about *Virginius,* 81-82, 83, 84; negotiates with Sickles, 76-85; on liberalization of Spain, 123; overthrown, 118-20; problem with Conservative Party, 89
Castro, Minister of State: negotiations for reparations, 125-26; punishment of Burriel, 127
Céspedes, Carlos Manuel de: mentioned, 11; outbreak of Ten Years War, 7-8; president of Cuban republic, 10; sends Quesada to U.S., 25

(175)

Céspedes, Pedro de: execution, 46-47; paraded in Santiago, 44; signs on *Virginius,* 33

Clarendon, George William Frederick, fourth Earl of, 15, 75

Clark, W.H., 61

Cobright, A.L., 57

Conkling, Roscoe, 67

Cordova, Altamont de, 31, 48-49

Costilla, Dionisio, 39

Cox, Samuel S., 67

Crawford, John, 81

Creagh, Caroline de, 22

Creswell, John A.J., 15, 17, 61, 98

Crook, George W., 36

Cuba: annexationist sentiment, 12; belligerency question, 11, 12, 13-15, 16; dual U.S.-Cuban citizens, 10; guerrilla warfare, 9-10, history, 5-7; *Juntas* in U.S., 11, 16; race questions, 132-33; restriction on trade, 7; significance to U.S., 136; slavery, 6-7, 11-12; Ten Years War, 7-12, 136-37; U.S. interest in, 4, 5

Cushing, Caleb: and King Alfonso, 125; appointed minister to Spain, 122; arrives in Spain, 123; background, 122; meets Sickles in Paris, 123; negotiations for reparations, 123-26; opposes Cuban belligerency, 14; seeks punishment of Burriel, 127-28; views of *Virginius* affair, 120

Cushing, William 53

Dana, Charles A., 15, 64

Dana, Richard Henry, 130

Davis, J.C. Bancroft, 67-68, 70, 98, 99, 100

Davis, Richard Harding, xv

de Carvajal, José, see Carvajal, José de

de Céspedes, Carlos Manuel, see Céspedes, Carlos Manuel de

de Céspedes, Pedro, see Céspedes, Pedro de

de Cordova, Altamont, see Cordova, Altamont de

de Creagh, Caroline, see Creagh, Caroline de

de Horsey, A.F.R., 48-49

de la Cámara, Manuel, see Cámara, Manuel de la

Del Montaigne, John, 92

del Sol, Jesús: death, 47; joins *Virginius* expedition, 33; paraded in Santiago, 44; tried and executed, 45

Dent, Frederick, 70

Despatch, U.S.S., 109-12

de Varona, Adolfo, see Varona, Adolfo de

Dulce, Domingo, 8, 9

Dupuy de Lôme, Enrique, 137

Evans, Robley D., 135

Evarts, William 67, 71

Favorita, 110

Figueras, Estanislao, 23

Fish, Hamilton: abilities, 133-34; and legal status of *Virginius,* 101-02; and patronage, 17; and State Department, 4; appearance, 2; attitude toward Spanish republic, 60; background, 2-4; belligerency question, 13-14, 15, 16, 59; Cabinet meetings, 17, 57-58, 59, 61, 90-91, 98, 99, 100; cables Sickles for information, 60; death, 139; declines compromise settlement, 97-98; demands in U.S. ultimatum, 79; directs Sickles to close legation, 61; discusses diplomatic actions, 61-62; dispenses with Spanish salute to U.S. flag, 102; friendship with Polo, 58; hears Polo's report on legality of *Virginius* papers, 62-63; meets with Thornton concerning *Virginius,* 59; mentioned, xv; negotiates with Polo, 88; negotiations for reparations, 124-25; opposes Sickles's appointment to Madrid, 17; problems regarding *Virginius,* 73; protests executions, 60; punishment of Burriel, 127; reaction to *Virginius* affair, 63, 132-34; receives word of *Virginius* capture, 57; relations with press, 64-65; reports of executions, 57-58, 60, 62; retirement, 138-39; Sickles's resignation, 115-17; strategy toward Spain, 22; Thanksgiving protocol, 92-95; triumph in *Virginius* affair, 1; *Virginius* protocol, 98-100

Forbes, Paul, 13

Fortune, 112

Fry, Joseph: appears before Santiago court, 51-52; background, 35; execution, 52-53; family, 138; reaction to pursuit by *Tornado,* 40-41; reparations for family, 125; taken prisoner, 43; takes command of *Virginius,* 35

Garfield, James A., 97

Garrus, Alphonse, 52

Gladstone, William, 81

Godkin, Edwin L., 14, 72

Gomez, Maximo, 27

Gould, Jay, 22

Grant, John P., 49, 53

Grant, Ulysses S.: administration, 2; appointees, 138; Cabinet discusses diplomatic actions, 61-62; Cuban belligerency, 11, 12, 13-14; inauguration, 1-2; legal status of *Virginius,* 101-102; letters from veterans, 69-70; mentioned, xv, 57; negotiations for reparations, 124, 125; Sickles's resignation, 117; supports Sickles's appointment to Madrid legation, 17-18; tells Fish to wire Sickles to protest to Spanish government, 58; Thanksgiving protocol, 92-95; *Virginius* protocol, 98-100

Granville, George Granville Levenson Gower, second Earl of: Britain's

stand on U.S. position, 83; receives Layard's report on *Virginius,* 82; receives Thornton's report on *Virginius,* 70; urges Castelar to agree to U.S. demands, 90

Gratz, Simon, 105

Great Britain: *Alabama* claims, 15; enters *Virginius* dispute, 47-49; Geneva arbitration, 4; policy toward U.S., xvi; *Virginius* negotiations, 81-83, 87-88, 89-91, 97, 127-28

Greeley, Horace, 63

Hall, A. Oakley, 15

Hall, Henry C.: and reaction in Cuba to protocol, 102-03; demands return of prisoners, 106; Fish receives his message of *Virginius* capture, 57; mentioned, 44, 45, 46; sends news of executions, 60,62

Hanna, Mark, 134

Harris, J.C., 36

Hay, John, 21

Hoar, Ebenezer Rockwell, 14, 17

Hyde, Charles Cheney, 131

Indio, 104

Isabel de Catolica, 103

Isabel II, Queen of Spain: and Cuba, 7; exiled in Paris, 21-22; mentioned, 125, 133; overthrown, 8

Jefferson, Thomas, 5, 71

Johnson, Andrew, 20, 66

Johnson, Reverdy, 20

Jordan, Thomas, 11

Jovellar, Juan: and remaining captive prisoners, 106; and U.S.-Spanish protocol, 102-03, 104; mentioned, 78; receives word of executions, 47; returns to Cuba, 1875, 137; seeks compromise settlement, 97

Juárez, Benito, 25

Juniata, U.S.S., 69, 106-07

Kansas, U.S.S., 27, 29, 30, 59-60, 69

(177)

Key, Philip Barton, 18
King, Henry, 35, 40, 43
Kingsley, Charles, 13
Knight, Charles A., 107
Knight, Henry, 40

Layard, Sir Austin Henry: asks U.S. to
allow Spain time to comply, 90;
background, 81; meets with
Castelar about *Virginius,* 81-82,
83, 84; meets with Serrano, 89;
meets with Sickles, 82-83; negotiations for reparations, 124;
punishment of Burriel, 127-28;
receives news of execution of
British subjects, 81; reports to
Granville on *Virginius* negotiations, 82, 89
Lersundi, Francisco, 8
Longstreet, James, 66
López, Narciso, 6, 10
Lorraine, Sir Lambton: and remaining prisoners, 107; appearance,
49; meets with Burriel, 54;
reaches Santiago, 54; receives orders to sail, 49
Lowry, R.B., 104-05

Maceo, Antonio, 137
McKinley, William, 134
Maine, U.S.S., 135
Mantilla, Antonio, 124-25, 127
Marble, Manton, 14
Martos, Christin, 23
Monasterio, Angel Ortiz, 41-42
Moore, John Bassett: legality of
executions, 129; legality of *Virgin-
ius* seizure, 130-31
Mora, José Marie, 26
Morales Lemus, José, 7, 11, 12
Moran, Benjamin, 91, 115
Morning Star, 52
Morton, Oliver P., 97, 132
Motley, John Lothrop, 13
Murtaugh, W.J., 64

Navy, U.S.: in *Virginius* affair, 135;
question of preparedness, 59;

strength of, 68-69
Niobe, H.M.S., 49, 52, 54
Nunes, Robert, 53

Ossipee, U.S.S., 114
Ostend Manifesto, 17, 80

Palma, Estrada, 137
Panic of 1873, 65
Pardo, Ruiz, 41-42
Parkman, Francis, 13
Patterson, John F., 16, 25-26, 100,
101
Pavia, Don Manuel, 118-20
Pearne, Thomas H., 31, 62
Peck, Harry Thurston, xv
Pi y Margall, Francisco, 24, 133
Pierce, Franklin, 5
Pierrepont, Edwards, 67, 68
Pile, William A., 28-29
Pinckney, Thomas, 44
Pinckney's Treaty of 1795, 44, 76
Pizarro, 27
Polo de Barnabé, José: background,
58; legal status of *Virginius,*
62-63, 101-02; meets with Fish
concerning *Virginius,* 58-59;
negotiates with Fish, 88; receives
Fish's protests of executions, 60;
retires, 137; seeks compromise
settlement, 97; Thanksgiving pro-
tocol, 92-95; *Virginius* protocol,
98-100
Porter, David G., 68
Prescott, William H., 13
Press: reaction to *Virginius* affair,
64-65, 72-73, 132; transition of
70s, 63-64; view of *Virginius* in
Spanish press, 83-84; views on
U.S. Navy, 69
Prim, Juan, 13, 22
Public opinion on *Virginius* affair,
65-68, 69-70, 72-73, 103

Quesada, Manuel: and early *Virginius* cruises, 28-29; arrives in
Washington, 25; background, 25;
joins *Virginius,* 26; mentioned, 9,

10, 11; owner of *Virginius*, 26; tried and sentenced, 45

Quesada, Rafeal, 66

Quesada, Ramon, 101

Rawlins, John 12, 13, 17

Reed, Allen V., 29, 30

Republican Society of Cuba and Puerto Rico, 7

Roberts, J.K., 25, 26, 101

Roberts, López, 58

Roberts, Marshall O., 25

Robeson, George: directed to assemble Navy, 61-62; mentioned, 57; Naval preparedness, 59; *Virginius* protocol, 98, 99

Rodgers, Lieutenant Commander, 109-10

Ryan, George Washington: actions on eve of execution, 46; background, 33-35; defiant attitude, 43; execution, 46-47; in Jamaica, 36; paraded in Santiago, 44; tried and executed, 45

Ryan, William, see Ryan, George Washington

Sagasta, Don Mateo, 22, 23

Santa Rosa, Agustin, 33

Schmitt, Emil G.: American vice-consul in Santiago, 44; attempts to aid prisoners, 44-45; meets with Burriel, 45-46; protests to Burriel, 45; wires Hall of Burriel meeting, 46; witnesses march of crew to execution, 52

Schroeder, Seaton, 29

Schurz, Carl, 132

Scott, Edward, 36, 43

Scott, James Brown, 130

Serrano, Francisco: and Conservative Party, 89; meets Cushing, 123; punishment of Burriel, 127

Seward, William H., 4

Sheppherd, Francis, 26, 100

Sheridan, Philip, 92

Sherman, John, 134, 135

Sherman, William T., 57, 69

Sickles, Daniel: as minister to Spain, 20-24; background, 18-20; basis for actions in Madrid, 80; death, 138; directed to take orders from Washington, 91; friendship with Grant, 20; later career, 138; meets Cushing in Paris, 123; meets with Layard, 82-83; message on *Virginius* capture, 57; negotiations in Spain, 75-85; official protest, 60, 79; ordered to prepare legation for closing, 61; proposed for legation in Madrid, 17; receives instructions to close legation, 79; receives Spanish agreement, 91-92; resignation, 115, 117, 118; Thanksgiving protocol, 94; U.S. press reaction to resignation, 117-18; views on Spanish actions regarding *Virginius* affair, 89-90; views on Spanish republic, 75-76

Sickles, Teresa, 18, 21

Smith, Charles, 28-29, 101

Spain: Carlists and revolution, 23; Cuban policies, 7, 11; 1868 revolution, 8; monarchy reestablished, 125; public opinion toward republic, 73; public reaction to *Virginius* surrender, 118; republican government, 22-24, 118; seeks compromise settlement, 97; U.S. attitudes toward, 12-13

Spanish-American War, see War of 1898

Steinway Hall, 70-71

Sumner, Charles: and foreign policy, 149; background, 71; mentioned, 2; views of *Virginius* crisis, 71-72, 132

Sunsunegeri, Evaristo Sanchez, 37

Thornton, Edward: asks Fish to give Spain more time, 87-88; meets with Fish, 59; reports on U.S. public opinion, 70; reports to Fish on British diplomacy in Spain, 90; seeks compromise settlement, 97; U.S. reaction to *Virginius*, 66;

Virginius surrender to U.S., 117
Tornado: crew boards *Virginius,* 42-43; construction, 39; fires on *Virginius,* 41; sighted by *Virginius,* 38; sights *Virginius,* 39-40; takes *Virginius* crew as prisoners, 43
Tyler, F.A., 112-14

Ulloa, Augusto, 123, 124
Underwood, E.B., 112-14

Varona, Adolfo de, 101
Varona, Bernabé, see Bembetta
Village Belle, 39, 40, 43
Villeva, Edwards, 61
Virgin, see *Virginius*
Virginia Seymour, 26
Virginius: and belligerency question, 59; arrives in Santiago, 43-44; as cause of Spanish-American War, xv; begins Cuban expedition, 33-38; boarded by *Tornado* crew, 42-43; condition when surrendered to U.S., 111-14; construction, 25; crew executed, 52-53; crew in prison, 105-107; early career, 26-31; international legal status, 94; international reaction to seizure, 87; legality of papers, 62; legality of seizure, 129-31; New York investigation, 100-02; protocol of surrender, 98-100; public opinion of seizure, 65-70,

72-73; purchase, 25-26; reaction of Fish to capture, 63; reaction of press to *Virginius* affair, 64-65, 72-73; remembered in 1890s, xv; response to escape attempt, 40-41; right to fly U.S. flag questioned, 60; sighted by *Tornado,* 39-40; significance, 129-37; sinking, 114; status under American law, 26; struck by *Tornado* gunfire, 41; surrender to U.S., 103-04, 109-11; word of capture reaches Fish, 57
Virginius affair in American history, 1, 136
Voice of America, 7
Volunteers: anti-U.S. sentiment, 11; origins, 8; policies, 8-9, 10
La Voz de Cuba, 9

Wall Street, 68
War of 1898, 131-33, 134-36
Washburne, Elihu, 118
Webster, Sidney, 14, 100
Whiting, W.D., 109-10
Williams, George H., 101-02
Wilson, Henry, 71
Woodrow, D.C., 112-14
Woolsey, Theodore D., 131
Wyoming, U.S.S., 48, 53

Young America, 5, 15
Young, J.D., 31
Young, William S., 53